CALLA PRESS 2023

CALLA PRESS 2023

Spring Issue

CALLA PRESS

Calla Press

Samantha Cabrera
Founder and Editor

Erin Samples
Editorial Assistant

Leslie Bustard
Communications Coordinator

Cover Art by Shannon Armstrong
Artist
@shannonarmstrong.art
Etsy @SArmstrongCollection

www.callapress.com
Calla Press

Contents

A Letter from the Editor

Dear reader,

I have been praying for this journal to make its way into your hands; as our second print journal, it is a humble task that we present to you over 50 authors ready and willing to open their tables for you, to read, explore, and be filled with immeasurable hope and longing for the things of Christ. One of my favorite authors, Douglas Kaine McKelvey writes the most poignant words from *Every Moment Holy*, "A Liturgy before Beginning a Book":

Let all things, and this book as well,
be tools in your hands,
to shape me and make me more truly your own,
more fitly a child of the hope
of the restoration of all things in Christ
whose fullness dwells within them.

So let the honest responses
of my heart to this reading
grant new insight into the story
your grace is already telling in my own life
that I might be a more willing co-laborer
in that process.

My prayer is that this small collection amidst the millions of books out in this world would point you toward the present love of The Father; the mission of Calla Press is to use the broken, after all, to tell the *holy*.

I have been privileged to read over numerous submissions for this journal; I have been wooed by their work as it has drawn me closer to Christ in ways I did not expect. I am humbled to present to you both established and emerging writers within this year's journal.

You will be taken to the floors of a hospital room full of weeping to the joys of gathering around a picnic table; it's a gift to be taken on a journey of words to a world the author created to bring a sense of order, peace, and understanding in a very chaotic, sorrowing, and hurried world. Grab some tea and pull up a chair, friend.

Love,
Samantha Cabrera
Editor

This book is dedicated to Leslie Bustard, for her willingness to serve Calla Press and her impactful contributions to the literary arts.

I

God in the Details by Debra Fiscus

Ceiling made from patches
of pine, oak leaves, and blue sky
carefully picked and placed
like perfect, broken stained glass
on white-steeple windows.

Chickadees flutter
from branch to branch, sucking
sweet wine from black raspberries
as crimson droplets dribble
down starch white breasts.

Trout lilies grow, drinking
sunshine leaked through ceiling cracks,
donning fine, silk skirts He provides.

They neither toil nor spin,
but their petals still grow.

Here, I come to worship, kneeling
on yellow trout lilies and feather mosses
before an altar of black cherry trees,
hiding blood-stained planks
behind flaking skin.

Here, I pray, doubting His plan
as chickadees play in the berries
and honeybees float from lily to lily,
living day after day, knowing
God is in the details.

2

Promised Land by Alexandria Marrow

Some mornings, your sister and I sit at the kitchen table,
sharing a quiet breakfast of toast and jam.
These mornings are a balm she won't remember.
Some evenings, your father speaks to you,
eyes weepy at the things you already make him feel.
These evenings are tonics I will remind him to drink
when you are older and exhausting.
Some afternoons, your kicks gently remind me
of small miracles happening everywhere,
each with intent and purpose.
Soon you will see this.
These daily blessings, both unremarkable and wondrous.
The love that begets you is a fragrance
you will soon be baptized in.
It fills up every room.

<h1 style="text-align:center">3</h1>

Drawing Near to Those with Mental Illness by Lara d'Entremont

Growing up, I heard adults whisper about people with "nerve" problems. I sat off to the side, fiddling with a loose thread on the couch, while the adults talked in hushed tones assuming the seven-year-old girl in pigtails wasn't paying much attention to them.

"She's always had bad nerves," one said, taking a sip of her coffee.

The other woman nodded. "Yes, I've heard she's on nerve pills, too."

"It's such a shame, really," the first said with a sigh. She crossed her legs. "I feel bad for her children. There she is, sitting in bed all day while her elderly parents take care of the children—and *her*. They don't need that. She just needs to get up and push through. She needs to stop this foolishness and take care of her family."

"And her poor husband," the second replied as she shook her head. "It's all a shame."

A shame, I thought. I paddled my pale feet dangling from the sofa. I worried a lot. I worried about poison hidden in my food, so I carefully inspected every bite and discarded any broken puffs of cereal. I checked my bathroom cupboards and shower every night before bed—or else I couldn't sleep. I had to pray the exact same prayer every night so nothing bad happened. I had to knock the creepy doll's head over each day to protect myself from monsters. Nausea caused me to scream, cry, sweat, and hyperventilate because I feared to vomit. Many nights, I laid awake in silent tears while sweat tingled on my neck as unwanted, inappropriate thoughts and images cycled in my head no matter how hard I fought to suppress them. *Do I have nerve problems?*

I didn't ask and I wouldn't find out for another eighteen years— when doctors put me on those unspeakable nerve pills.

* * *

One lunch hour in high school, I hid a friend's lunchbox and pretended I didn't know where it was. My friend snickered at me. "Oh Lara, you are truly the worst liar. You'll never be able to tell a good lie." I laughed along with her. *If only you knew.*

By grade 1, I mastered how to suffer levels 6, 7, and 8 panic attacks silently after a teacher criticized me for "acting foolish" during snack time. I taught myself how to cry noiselessly in the bathroom and fix my appearance to look unchanged. I fulfilled my compulsions where no one watched. I became an expert in my body language to mask every nuance that could give away my true feelings.

To make any excuse readily available to cover for situations where my emotions poked through my shell, I wrote a mental list of lies: *I'm hot; I just need some fresh air. I ate something weird yesterday. I stayed up late last night doing homework, so I'm a bit tired and zoned out today. I can't go to the movies today; I don't have a ride.* And the ever classic: "I'm fine—truly," with a chuckle for good measure.

Meanwhile, publicly emotional people confused me. Why did they let their tears flow so freely? Didn't they know that those who were comforting them now would later mock them behind their back? At the same time, I yearned for connection. I wanted someone to see my tears and wipe them away. I wanted someone to cradle me in their arms. But how could I trust them? I knew what people did when you had "nerve problems." The risk was too dangerous.

But suppressing can only last so long. Emotions don't go away and they will be seen, heard, and dealt with—one way or another.

* * *

At twenty-four years old, I paced the living room floors with my shoulders hunched up around my neck. We were in the midst of a family crisis that had turned my world upside down; it began the night before, but the reality of its repercussions settled in the following morning with intense anxiety.

I clenched my hands so tight that my nails dug into my palms and bled. My tongue was sore from the pressure of my teeth. I let my thirteen-month-old twins out of the gated living room to quiet their screams, but one continued crying. His noise heightened the anxiety welling up inside. I had to stop the crying, but nausea threatened to send my breakfast back up on the floor, and panic tensed every muscle in my body. I couldn't help him.

Help is coming. I'll tell them I'm tired and need to lie down. You can get over this and finish out the day strong. I recited this as I walked in front of the window. I watched and listened for Toni's silver-green car to pull into the driveway. Since the twins' birth, we'd hired Abbi and her mom Toni to help during the weekdays, but today both of them were coming to help.

I missed them pulling in but heard the back door open. My breath shook. My feet scrambled over each other to the porch. "Hi— I'm sorry—I'm really tired—the kids were up a lot—I just need to lay down."

"It's fine," Toni said, as she and her daughter peeled off their winter layers of boots and jackets. "This is a hard time, and we're here to help."

I nodded and retreated to the bedroom before they could say more.

I ran into my room and curled up on the bed. I contained my panic attack without a sound as it burst and rose to a ten. I suffered through it as quietly as I could, knowing it had to come down eventually. And it did. With sweat gleaming on my skin, I finally sat on my bed and wept.

It was a hard time. It was an *unreal* hard time. I dreamt at night that reality was merely a nightmare and my life had gone back to normal—but each morning I woke up and realized the opposite was true. There was no tangible end in sight to stretch towards. I suffered through the day with a stupid smile on my face and collapsed each evening into tears and more panic. I felt like I was free falling through a dark hole as a rope whistled past me. The light at the top grew smaller and smaller each morning. Stuffing panic attacks become more and more untenable.

I stood up and listened to the noises outside my room; I heard the whisk of the broom over the vinyl kitchen floor and the twins' soft giggles in the living room.

I crept out of the bedroom. I pulled my unkempt, tousled hair back with a headband. I still wore my sweat-stained pajamas—an old, stretched-out t-shirt with faded shorts. The only person I ever allowed to be this way was my husband—*never* Toni and Abbi. I inched into the kitchen anyway. I practiced the conversation in my head: I would tell them I needed a shower and would be out in a moment to take over. I stepped out of the shadows of the hallway and met Toni's brown eyes.

My emotions burst from within my shell. Like the snap of a rope stretched too taut, something splintered within me. Sobs lurched out of me. Toni came to my side and drew me into her arms. I kept my arms bundled across my chest but sunk in her hug.

"I'm so sorry," she whispered as she stroked my hair. "I can't imagine the pain and grief you feel right now." She remained quiet as she held me and I wept.

When the tears slowed, she pulled back slightly to look me in the eyes. I braced myself. I waited for her to tell me how much my kids needed me and how I had to pull myself together in order to help them process this difficult time. I had to hold up this family and I couldn't let my nerves get the best of me now.

But she didn't.

"Lara," she whispered. "Today, I don't want you to worry about the kids—Abbi and I have it all under control. Your children will be taken care of. I don't want you to worry about the housework because we've got that covered too. And we've got meals arranged for the rest of the week."

I stared at her.

She continued. "Today, I want you to take care of *you*. If that means you stay in the bedroom, that's okay. You need to process and you need to take care of yourself. Your presence, though welcome, isn't needed here. It's all under control. You do what you need to do. It's okay to cry and feel everything that you're feeling. You need to do that. It's okay; anyone in your position would feel this way right now."

New tears formed in my eyes. She had no harsh judgment. She cared. She understood. And she wanted me to get better—not stuff the grief down.

The following morning, I came out of my room to find Toni.

I cycled through another major panic episode and retreated to my room while she and her daughter cared for my kids. My tangled hair had bobby pins hanging out here and there, and my grubby pajama shirt smelled of body odor. I found Toni playing with Legos with my toddler in his bedroom. This time I knew the hard truth would come. She allowed one adult meltdown, but it was time to pull it together. I prepared for a lecture.

She saw me and stood up from the floor. She put her hands on me and looked into my eyes. "What do you need, Lara? We are here to help you."

I felt tears stinging my eyes again. "I'm so sorry for not taking care of my—"

She put a hand up. "No, Lara. Don't ever apologize for this." At that moment, she covered me with love. Her words extended to me like hands adorned in grace; where I couldn't hold my world together anymore, she sought to be my scaffolding. She taught me gentleness with the broken—even when it's our own souls that are quivering and weak.

* * *

From that point on, I began extending new gentleness and kindness to my emotions. As I did, I still cycled between panic and utter numbness. After the panic dissolved and the numbness settled in, the anxiety always returned like an unforeseen whirlwind and knocked me down.

However, in the following days as I remembered Toni's compassion, I mustered up the strength to shower and help with lunch. Some evenings I'd cry inconsolably, and Toni would drive to my home to sit with me. One morning I called her as panic overwhelmed me before I could even get out of bed. She soothed me each time, taking as long as I needed. Day by day, I got better. I learned to speak with self-compassion towards myself—just as Toni spoke to me.

I think often about that mom with the "nerve problems" I heard the adults talking about that day all those years ago. Did anyone show her compassion? Did anyone show her the kind of love I received? For all the adults that criticized her and gossiped behind her back, did one ever step into her home to simply love her in her time of need?

When someone suffers cancer, grief, job loss, or the like, we have a better idea of what to do. We bring meals, offer childcare, provide gifts, send flowers and cards, and sit with them. But when mental illness debilitates a family, we feel at a loss for how to help.

I think of how Jesus drew near to the broken, the diseased, the sick, and the ailing. While Jesus had scathing words for hypocrites like the religious leaders, he came with a different tone to the hurting and repentant. Though people tried to silence and keep the blind man away from Jesus, Jesus called out for him to be brought near. Though the bleeding woman tried to receive her healing without bothering Jesus, he made a point of noticing and speaking to her. Though the leprous man knelt before Jesus and said, "If you are willing, you can make me clean," Jesus reached out and touched him to make him clean. Jesus drew near.

Like Jesus, Toni drew near to me in my suffering. She didn't stand at a distance to whisper about me. She didn't scold me. She embraced me, cared for my home, loved my children, and sat with me through panic attacks. She showed me compassion and mercy and in turn, showed me how Christ's love is even greater. Where I feared his angry scowl for my behavior, I realized his kindness through her.

From one who has suffered the pillaging of her mind by mental illness—and watched the same happen to her loved ones—here's how we can help those who are suffering from mental illness: Resist the whispers of gossip and speculation. Reach out and show them compassion and, in turn, you might teach them how to give compassion to themselves. You may image Christ for them. That's the greatest gift you can give anyone who battles mental illness.

4

The Sower by R. L. Busséll

"Listen! A sower went out to sow." Matthew 13:3

See the sower who sows with abandon:
who pays no heed to where the seed will fall.
Some fall among the thorn, the stone, the dun,
some fall near where the airy birds will sprawl,
some fall on soil as rich as Eden-fair;
yet the heedless sower's still flinging wide
all the seed his pouch contains—none to spare.
Where do I stand in your tale, O my Guide?
Am I the soil of shallow heart and mind?
Am I the thorny-one that chokes and chides?
Am I the stone that envies green—the blind?
Do I dwell where the black-eyed bird resides?
O quench Your sword! I would dwell in Eden.
I would call on Christ. I would cross the Jordan.

5

the already and the not-yet
by Emma Michael

If I didn't believe in God I'd believe in
a universe that could laugh at me—could
understand my soft spots and
sorrows and tweak the day-to-day to
augment my brokenness for that kind
of pleasure that comes from plucking
powdery wing after wing from the
butterfly but

since I do believe in God
I must believe that somewhere somehow, in
all of these splinters and fruit peels,
there is life to take hold of and hope
to claim   there is a man who drank my
wrath cup dry and who knew this world meant suffering yet

still came to redeem it   a man I can know
with increasing clarity as I travel these
un-weed whacked footpaths and who
has wrapped me in promises of titanium and
silk   I must believe
there is a user of my sin and hurt and that
He is a master of turning fissures upside-
out and can
hasten believing to seeing
even for eyes yet to be resurrected

6

Fall, World, but Come to Rest by Stephanie Gail Eagleson

fall, world, but come to rest:
the ever-careful taker has
cradled all the grains of soul
in his embryonic hope chest,
inverted hourglass turned out upon itself,
and set to count the moments till
the dust has settled,
your ash becoming flesh.

7

To Sleep by Dani Nichols

His little head is covered with brown curls, which I futilely attempt to comb above his cute tan ears and deep brown eyes. His favorite things are animals that go "rawr!", tractors and his blankie, a tiny green square of fleece, printed with dinosaurs and grubby from being carried everywhere.

At two years old, he's not a good sleeper, but to be fair, he never has been; he'd rather stick with the rocking and lullabies and skip the going-to-sleep part altogether. But when we met him for the first time, he was asleep, in that hours-old newborn dream state, lying swaddled in a tiny plastic crib in his birthmother's hospital room—all five pounds of him. She nodded at us and we exchanged pleasantries. I couldn't take my eyes off him, it felt so odd to be chatting while he lay there, after all, he was the bridge between our wildly variant lives, he was the mighty force of change in a many-times-washed cotton swaddle. After a moment, she seemed happy for us to take him to a room down the hall, and especially relieved to be requesting a cheeseburger from the social worker, who'd offered to pick up food from a local diner. We were all searching for comfort in our own ways. We all needed sustenance.

The maternity ward was nearly empty, so the staff kindly offered me a vacant room. It wasn't the kind of hospital where you chose to have babies if you could help it, of course, we couldn't help it. It was in a troubled neighborhood, the streets lined with trash and graffiti, gunshots a common percussion to the discordant melody of bus horns and loud voices. The nurses all smiled at me knowingly as I gently rocked this little person, whose birth mother and father went outside to smoke cigarettes, openly flaunting the ward rules.

Our first adoption had been different, we'd met our daughter's birth family in a rushed and emotional encounter, not even allowed a photo with them before they were gone and we were thrust through the pale enclosure of the Newborn Intensive Care Unit (NICU) with a child, who, grace upon grace, was now a healthy and lively toddler. This time, the birth family wanted our presence. They seemed relieved that we'd come to help, that we were carefully non-judgmental about their bad habits, their family complexities, and their addictions.

The first night, I stayed in the borrowed room with the baby we hoped would be ours, and my husband, Adam, went to the rental house with our precocious two-year-old girl, who had about as much patience for quiet hospital rooms as you would expect. I laid down in the uncomfortable hospital bed and put my hand on the slowly rising and falling chest of this baby, still in his Tupperware-like crib. Around 3 a.m., a time I am now accustomed to, they took him into the nursery for tests, and after an hour or so of snoozing I decided to check on him. There was a loud beeping from the nursery and nurses were running, not frantically, not how I felt, but with purpose in their brave faces and soft-soled steps. I over-heard "withdrawal" and "he needs to go to St Josephs" the only local hospital with a NICU. This feeling was familiar, I knew it must be my baby. But they weren't obligated to tell me, I wasn't even on documentation yet, and I was not a legal guardian or a relation. I was a ghost mother, a non-entity who stood by to have her heart ripped out off-screen.

I wobbled at the window to the nursery and felt my heart puddle at my feet and then climb back up my legs to run around frantically in my chest for a few beats before dropping down and glopping about again. I wanted to sit down, hit something, and call someone. They told me to get away from the window and I did so, standing nervously to the side and staring at the boring, abstract art on the beige walls. I finally texted Adam, "I think something might be wrong," an understatement but all I knew to say.

Finally, after years (or maybe it was an hour?) a nurse came out and smiled at me. "You're the adoptive mom for the little guy born yesterday morning, right?"

"Yes," I quivered.

"Sorry for all that," she said. "It was a scramble, we had another little fella born on drugs, and he needed a NICU. But yours is doing great. Come in and see him."

My heart re-constituted from its puddled state and took up residence in its rightful place again. I smiled what I hoped was a grin of confident motherhood and followed her into the nursery.

A few hours later, his birth parents signed the adoption paperwork, a day early. They told us *thank you*, held him briefly, and without fanfare they were gone. Suddenly, we were the only parents present for him, the only ones to wake him. We held him close with the odd combination of grief and gratitude which accompanies adoption.

This morning, I heard my baby wake up, him of the frowsy curls and dinosaur love, and since it was 3 a.m., I groaned with irritation. After two years we often lose patience with early wake-up calls and middle-of-the-night cries of "Mama! Dada!" as he holds his blankie and clings to the edge of the crib, stomping his little feet in sleepy fear.

But I shuffle into his room and my crankiness melts away when he reaches his chubby arms up to be held. He nestles his head into my chest, and snuffles and sighs in contentment, glad to hear my heartbeat, to know I'm there. When the sun rises and the day begins, he is our fearless little farm boy, eager to help daddy on the tractor and chase his sister and hug our very tolerant dog and cat. But in the wee hours, he needs the reassurance of steady pulses and calm voices, the presence of people who are safe, who aren't going anywhere.

At my best, I tell him I remember. I remember how worried I was, how worried he might still be. I hold him and tell him the story of how much we love him, that, as his big sister says, "When I was tiny baby, mommy, and daddy got on a big plane and came to get me, and I was very brave and got on a plane too. When baby bruffer was a tiny baby, we did it again!"

What joy in her telling of a painful and not always clear-cut story, what grace to glimpse it simply, undressed with our grown-up fears and nuance.

He will know his story, both the childish, innocent version and the complicated, messy truths. He will know his beginning was uncertain, there were reasons he didn't sleep well. But he'll also know that even broken beginnings are beautiful, that he has two sets of parents who love him enough to do what's right for him, to let him go or to rock him through the night.

8

Prayers before Faith by Lee Kiblinger

Are prayers before faith phrases falling,
mist-like, evaporating to the ground—
waves of words echoed empty, hollow,
voiced but lost, just unheard sound?
Are cries crammed into cardboard boxes,
never opened in attics of dust—
pleas planted as seeds of what-ifs
in deserts windblown by sandy trust?
Do they move molecular, atoms combining
waiting for rising, concussive heat—
or hang like stars, with hope aligning
that forecast victory or herald defeat?
Do they come of age and ripen
like wild berries full of sweetened juice—

or are words wrapped up, cocoonlike,
until they warm, and then fly loose?

Their holding pattern is a mystery,
Still their wonder will incubate—
past utterance to future litany,
learned, rehearsed after timeless wait.

9

The Gift of Her Silence by Sandy Brannan

She had lived the way she always talked. Pithy was the only word I ever used to describe it, but I suppose someone who knows more about words than I do might come up with a better expression to describe her. There was just something quick and forceful about her, something that always left you wanting more. But she only gave what she gave, not a bit more, and somehow, over the years we were friends, I learned to accept it.

When her daughter called me yesterday, I instantly felt a pain in my stomach that shouldn't have been there. But, like my heart, my stomach somehow knew what had happened even before I heard the words.

How very like her to die that way. Just to sit down, close her eyes, and go away. No fancy preamble, no attempt to draw things out, not even a single goodbye.

Now all I can do is think about the words she never spoke, words I desperately want to hear to help crowd out the painful thoughts coursing through my mind. I can't help but wonder about her thoughts, she never seemed to have much to say yet still managed to leave long-lasting impressions on those she came into contact with.

I sit here, uncomfortably comfortable in my chair, and ponder if I said enough. I never followed her lead because being quiet has never been my strength. After all, what she lacked in words I had in spades. She would grant me a subtle smile once in a while, but she mostly seemed to ignore me as I spoke. Having been her friend for nearly four decades, I knew she listened to every single word I said. Somehow we had clicked, growing stronger together as each year of our friendship passed us by.

Still, as I rest my head on the cushion of the chair she preferred every time she came for a visit, I can't help but wish for a second chance to tell her more.

Her daughter has asked for my help, and has asked me to take charge of the service and the days leading up to it. I know what she's really asking me to do, and I just don't know if I can. How do you take a lifetime and sum it up? Even if I had time to waste and every word ever uttered at my disposal, I still couldn't share what she meant to me, what I suspect she meant to all of us.

So, I'll take my cue from her. Relief washes over me as I finally have my answer. I can't help but smile, even though I don't think anyone would be able to see it on my face, as I reach for my notebook and pen. I know I won't be writing for long. I know I will think of only a few things to jot down that I'll use when I stand beside her one last time.

I tell myself I won't cry, that she wouldn't want tears on her shiny coffin soon to be covered with the dirt that she loved to thrust her hands into every spring. The deep earthy smell would cling to her long after the beautiful flowers sprang forth like an offering. I know now I'll never see another flower without thinking about her.

I tell myself I'll remember how much she managed to say even when her lack of words left me wanting more. It hurts me to realize how much she said without speaking, the opportunities to know her better that I let slip past me. I'll give her what she would have wanted, but my words will betray my voice as I force most of them to stay deep inside my heart. No one will notice but me. I can't help the chill that forces itself over my body as I finally understand how often she felt the same way.

Closing the notebook, I slowly make my way out of my chair toward the phone. I need to let her daughter know everything will be fine. I'll say the words her mother said to her time and time again, even though we both know we'll never quite be the same. I'll say just enough to comfort her, holding back everything that would invariably make me feel better. It might be the first truly unselfish conversation I've ever had.

As I listen to the phone ring on the other end of the line, I'm grateful I'm alive. I know she would want me to help her child heal. Even though she never asked me to do it, I know she would want me to slowly pour out everything about our friendship, allowing the slow release of words over time to heal the tender hearts of the ones she left behind.

I used to think it was strange how two women, so very different, could be so close. Now I see that it was always part of a bigger plan.

I can hear the tears in her daughter's voice as she answers the phone. Her pain echoes my own, but I do what I now know my friend always did for me. I give her part of my strength as I share a few simple words with her. As I speak, I can feel her daughter relax and I know she'll be okay.

It surprises me how much my friend is still teaching me. Turns out I have a lot to think about. We hang up; I go to get ready for bed. I'm grateful for the silence.

10

My Childhood Home by Matthew J. Andrews

(after Scott Erickson's *House of Belonging*)

I took a walk by it today,
found it abandoned, decrepit,
termites eating the wood, wind
ripping away the shutters, shards of glass.

There was a hole in the roof,
a thick redwood reaching up,
wider than I could ever embrace,
the canopy a dense shade of green,

the bark warm like molded clay,
families of birds chattering stories
to each other on strong branches.
I walked inside to inspect the roots;

the house was no longer locked
because there was no longer a door,
just fresh air flowing in and out,
as if the old house could finally breathe.

grace be by Marianna Pizzini Mankle

I stand
with open hands and outstretched
arms, but this is not
a present I can hold.
and I have never stared at
bloodstained gowns and
nail-ripped palms
while accepting a gift.
praise be to you who
saw me,
chose me,
and granted me
unending love,
even after betrayals
that left you crying out

in pain,
in anguish,
in death.
you offer grace abundant without
bows or wrapping
paper, and while my hands
shake and my heart quakes,
you stand
steady,
firm,
and founded.
grace be given to me,
undeserved.

I2

Palm Sunday by Linda McCullough Moore

Wondering
at the palm fronds
shaken at the donkey's head.
Brusque tribute, I have always thought,

and perhaps not
just a bit
annoying.

Was the green wave
cry for help or accolade.

Is there a difference.

A hundred would-be
indie rock stars
at a football game
sing Hallelujah,
preachers strutting,
coiffed and praising,
on the take;
stalwart pilgrims earnest
till they're not.

Take time out
of your busy week
to watch church on TV.
Or scatter branches at his feet,
throw down your clothes
in Old Jerusalem.
It is all one, I think

and have to wonder
how that deaf-making,
rabble-roused, and heartfelt
- say it - tribute
struck the Lord.

Jesus, how did it feel to you?

Prescient.
Already weary.
Eye on the turning.

13

Entering A Dark Season by Caity Neuberger

This will probably be one of the hardest, but best, seasons of your life," my older brother and his wife were telling me. "It has been for us."

It was my thirtieth birthday, and my brother (ten years my senior) had called to congratulate me, offer wisdom, and share some laughs about our respective children. After our conversation, I remember jotting down a few takeaways: "Hardest. Best. Don't be discouraged. Long, difficult, growing decade." These notes felt vital and somehow full of hope, like looking at a map that someone had drawn up of their own journey through a place that I was about to enter. There might be sinking sand and dragons and deceitful cities full of riches ahead, but hey, at least I would know about it ahead of time, right?

Little did I know that things would begin their downward slope only a few hours later.

The day after my birthday, I got my wisdom teeth pulled. Normally this experience happens in your late teens or early twenties—not when you turn thirty and already deal with daily fatigue from taking care of all your small children. But I'm a late bloomer in many respects, so waiting to hit this "milestone" was perfectly in character.

The first two days post-surgery went alright; my family pitched in to help, the "good" pain meds kept me from feeling most of the pain and discomfort, and I fully rested without entertaining a smidgen of guilt. But then that semi-blissful state wore off, and I struggled to maintain my composure. My pain increased and ibuprofen only helped minimally. Eating became a chore. The rest of my family moved on with their normal lives, and I stayed stuck in aches and pains. Then two of my kids got fevers and runny noses.

As the environment in our home intensified over the next three days, I found myself crying out to God a lot. All sorts of things bubbled up to the surface:

How much longer will I be in pain?

Why is this happening—what good is coming out of this?

I'm not doing anything good or useful. What a waste of time.

Why do we all feel so terrible?

Is it okay for us to watch this much TV right now? And if so, why?

All I want to do is sleep and wake up when this is over.

As I continued to cry out to God, he kept meeting my anxiety with stillness: a non-urgent response to my rattling struggle. I kept asking him what he wanted me to *do*, but he continued to apply the gentle pressure of, "Stay still. Don't move." I tried to relax into his good plans and his good hands, but my desire to earn my way into good things in life wrestled hard with his command. The clock seemed to keep track of the endless hours in which I was both unproductive and unwell.

Sit still? When it hurts? God, you want me to let this pain take over, let these days be slow and crappy, let things go on as they are without trying to change or fix it at all?! This is useless and pointless and I feel like a worthless human being right now!

Then both sides of my surgery site became infected, and I was put on more antibiotics and medicine. I had to put up a chart on our whiteboard because I couldn't keep track of what I should be taking and when. I'm that crunchy, homeopathic girl that reaches for a cup of water and her essential oils before ever thinking of touching the medicine cabinet, so having a "medication schedule" grated on my every last nerve. Conventional medicine? Not my thing. But the pain was driving me towards compliance; in order to function (which required caring for four children, ages two-to-six), I needed to take the pills. So I did.

There was one night when the pain woke me at three-thirty in the morning. I snuck downstairs, aware of every single creak of our floorboards, and pulled out my phone while I waited for the ibuprofen to kick in so I could sleep again. As I perused Instagram, I came across this photo, dark and plain and anything but flashy. The words scrawled across it read:

"Make a peaceful nightly ritual of being silent before God" (quote by Lysa Terkeurst).

I set down my phone and I sat still in the darkness. A cricket or two was humming just outside. The curtains, draped across our living room windows, seemed soft and graceful, their shadows lined with moonlight glowing just beyond my vision. The clock ticked calmly—this time not reminding me of time lost, but of time gained. In these minutes of quiet, my heart poured forth a prayer of gratitude:

Dear God, thank you that I can sit here in pain and in the dark...and that that is enough for you. Enough for me.

God wasn't asking anything of me at this moment other than to be *in* it. To set aside my prideful planning, my anxious grasping, my people-pleasing overachieving, and my worried striving in order to sit in silence before a holy God who created me to endure such a moment as this.

In pain. In the dark.

I will be the first one to shy away from a blow, the first one to avoid any sort of pain or discomfort or embarrassment. Yet I know that these things work out something unique within our minds and bodies. When I have a headache, I don't reach for Tylenol. When I get sick, I don't reach for the cough syrup. I take more vitamins and drink more water and allow my body to go through it. Why? Because I know that God made my body go through this and come out on the other side of it a victor. When I prepared to give birth to my babies, one of the first things on my birth plan each time was "no pain medication." Why? I had researched what our bodies go through during labor, and I discovered that the pain during labor works all sorts of near-magical processes within our bodies. So I knew that God made my body to go through it and come out on the other side a victor.

Pain makes a way for joy. Feeling our pain (rather than numbing or hiding from it) allows miraculous changes to occur within us. Don't get me wrong, I was still popping pills to stay afloat during this whole wisdom-teeth saga. But they didn't take away the pain and frustration and worthlessness that I felt, and those feelings pressed me into Jesus in a new way.

I cannot compare my two-week brush with pain to the daily suffering experienced by many; how there is chronic hunger, nausea, loss, and debilitating pain being wrestled with even now. But no matter the level of discomfort we each may face, the invitation remains the same: *Come as you are. Come and be with Me.* We are drawn into God's presence as an act of love, and he longs to engage with us and offer peace to us, before we worry, complain, or try to fix our problems.

After the time spent at his feet, we are of course free to address our pain, share our burdens with others, look for ways we can operate in our current frustrating state, rest as needed, or find entertainment. Our God does not wish to take away these other things from us. Rather, he wants us to experience the fullness of his presence first—to get a taste of heaven in the midst of what feels like a living hell. To know that he is absolutely with us in our pain and certainly aware of it.

To sit in the dark. With the pain. No further efforts are necessary.

Dear friend, if God wants you to rise up and get to work, lay aside your suffering, and start serving, then he will push you gently towards that thing—and he will also confirm it. Satan is the one who uses fear and urgency to sharply prod us forward. But our God lovingly directs us and knows that we need both reminders and confirmations in order to continue following. Do not feel guilty about what you can or cannot "accomplish" today in your current season. He may simply be asking you to sit in the dark and rest with him.

After that night of stillness at Jesus's feet, things didn't get better or easier for me. In fact, they got *worse*. My family started dropping like flies—falling under the burden of fevers and headaches. Then just when I thought I was over my troubles with the infection, I woke up to a full-body rash, an allergic reaction to the antibiotic I was on. This rash persisted for two and a half days. Quickly following our pain, my husband became sick again.

The question, "Why, God?" was often on my lips, but I quelled that stunted, human way of thinking. I didn't need to know *why*. I just needed to know that there *was* a why, and that my God still loved me.

When you are in a dark or painful season, be in The Word. Be in prayer. But most of all, be willing to be silent in the darkness with the Lord, entrusting your pain and the reasons for it to our loving Father God.

14

Bones by Stephanie Nygaard

Your bones wear the marks
of youth,
pictures scribbled
in sheer innocence,
words etched
in pure delight.
Your flesh is colored in pastels—
lilac, celery, mist, pink.
You're clothed in
a robe of grey-green
to keep you warm
on wintery nights.
We fill you with
firelight,
music, and memories.

You, in turn,
envelop us in an embrace
of belonging.
Our stories are
ever entwined.
Our bones are stronger
because of yours.

15

The First Fall by Chelsea Barnwell

'Be fruitful,' how the gardeners have failed.
Leaves aflame, wrathful messengers of God.
We have eaten the fruit, death has been hailed.
God! We've killed it all! All returns to sod.
Earth brown and brittle, now we walk alone,
The chill wind stunts growth, even of the thorn.
We bury the seed, what can now atone?
Weeping, we see the earth of glory shorn.
Oh, spare us! Send life for we surely die!
Then tender, living, green, a shoot appears,
Buried, yet alive, answer to our cry,
Dead trees in flower, smiles amid tears.
You said my seed would crush the serpent's head.
What wonder that the seed first must be dead!

16

Jonah, Reluctant Prophet
by Meg Freer

Oh, that today you would listen to his voice,
harden not your hearts. (Psalm 95)

My heart hardened by the world,
its exhausting polyphony of voices,
no argument with God but flight
from His thunderstrike of breath,
from the daunting prospect
of converting the enemy, Ninevah.
Job's pride is mine too.

My avoidance of duty,
the sailors' murmurs and complaints
about the cause of the storm,
their layers of pain squeezed

from translucent shadows,
attempts to row to land,
their decision to throw me
into the primeval, surging ocean
an ugly *forte* but not revenge,
weight lifted from my shoulders
as I accept punishment.

The sea monster—a demon,
provider of destinies—already there
at Joppa, three days and nights
with me in its belly as it swam,
then a journey on the Tigris,
God's provision of the fastest route
from the Mediterranean to Ninevah,
and time for me to realign my purpose,
to realize that God intends salvation for all.

17

꩜

"She sweeps with many-colored Brooms": Reflections on the Poetry of Emily Dickinson by Kellie Brown

Regarded by some as The Belle of Amherst, the American poet and woman of letters Emily Dickinson can hardly be described by a single moniker. She remains a mystery, not fully knowable, and yet paradoxically revealed in intimate glimpses through her verse. Dickinson held words as sacred and the act of stringing them together as a solemn ritual undertaken with great reverence. Spending her entire life in Amherst, Massachusetts, Dickinson fashioned a stoic public persona that over time resembled a narrowing funnel that let in fewer and fewer people. She eventually chose to interact with those outside her family through letters. These epistolary relationships worked well because the reclusive Dickinson proved most expressive when applying ink to paper. But more importantly, she experienced life so intensely that it was sometimes hard for others to be near her. She found it even more difficult to be with herself at times.

> *The Soul selects her own Society—*
> *Then—shuts the Door—*
> *To her divine Majority—*
> *Present no more—...*

But no matter how confided her outer realm became, her inner life soared. She preferred to compose her poems during the night, but like any dedicated writer, was never without a scrap of paper and pencil throughout the day to record images, words, and phrases that came unbidden. Emily Dickinson found inspiration in the quotidian tasks of the day—"She sweeps with many-colored Brooms –...,"1 and crafted them, sometimes rather cryptically, into metaphors about life, death, faith, and the human condition. Grasping the preciousness of the temporal and the ephemeral, she commented on the stem of a dandelion, a gust of wind, a beam of light, the baptism of dew, and the drift of a dust moat. Not even the most seemingly inconsequential of our lives, such as the gnat, escaped her notice and contemplation.

I am not sure when I encountered my first Emily Dickinson poem, but I know that they have been roaming around in my mind for as long as I can remember. When I feel a longing for her words, I usually reach for the old paperback that has rested on the bookshelf of every home I've lived in for the past thirty-some years. The edges of its pages are soiled and slightly foxed, and the orange cover faded to pink. It fits nicely in my hands, neither too large nor too small, and the pages offer a satisfying crackling sound as I turn them. Published in 1961, this volume was not new when I received it from a dear friend during my freshman year of college. Both "preachers' kids," he and I shared an eclectic affinity for words, sounds, and images that rendered us a bit out of step with our high school peers. Rather than be concerned about our eccentricities, we relished in comfortable smugness during the long hours spent discussing poetry, listening to Mahler symphonies, watching the mesmerizing images of Philip Glass's *Koyaanisqatsi*, anticipating Marlon Brando's "Stella!" scream in *A Streetcar Named Desire*, and singing along with Gordon MacRae and Shirley Jones in *Oklahoma!*

My friend had found this particular volume of Emily Dickinson's poetry in some second-hand shop, and it fit into his budget as an impoverished college student. He proudly presented it to me as a Christmas present in 1989 with a beautiful note about our friendship inscribed on the title page. Priceless to me, this well-worn paperback will never land in the discard pile during a bookshelf culling. A few years ago, I lovingly tucked my favorite photo of us between two pages. It depicts one of our happy adventures as we stand near the Covered Bridge in Elizabethton, Tennessee, a historic structure built in 1882, four years before Emily Dickinson's death. We look impossibly young and relaxed. He is wearing his standard outfit: a well-washed T-shirt and Birkenstocks. My short-sleeved top is paired with black shorts and sunglasses. Leaning against a white wooden fence at the edge of the water where ducks swim and seek bread handouts, we smile at the camera, my friend's arm draped around my shoulder. For the first time recently, I wondered what passerby we asked to take our picture. But that will remain unknowable, almost as elusive as the recapturing of a wonder-filled day from one still photo, one fixed moment in time.

Emily Dickinson proved exceptionally dexterous at capturing a snapshot of a moment through words. Adjectives and adverbs painted a vivid portrait, while her deftly chosen verbs left much open to interpretation. She embraced minimalism way before it evolved into the admired alternate lifestyle championed by some today. She lived a life of minimal possessions and relationships, an ascetic landscape on which to create. She valued an economy of words, a frugality that came not out of scarcity but because she savored the plucking of that one perfect word that held a world of meaning within its few letters. She mostly preferred to communicate her poetic message in no more than 20 lines and never exceeded 50. Instead of epic narrative poems such as those by Keats or Byron, Dickinson offered her eventual readers imagery and veracity in concentrated capsules.

While her poems rested in a confined physical space on the page, Dickinson knew few bounds in her subject matter. She wrote much of nature, and the divine, and the relationship of both to the human condition. Her verse often spoke of hope, and so despite what limitations the world or even she herself imposed, it seemed that the light of hope burned brightly in her spirit.

> *"Hope" is the thing with feathers—*
> *That perches in the soul—*
> *And sings the tune without the words—*
> *And never stops—at all—...*

She did not shy from explorations of the eschatological kind because she felt a restlessness to know what happens at the end, what exists beyond the present life we know.

> *Before Me—dips Eternity—*
> *Before Me—Immortality—*
> *Myself—the Term between—...*

Her religious roots grew from the strict, piety-focused tradition of the Congregationalists. She tried as a young person to feel at home in that world and belief system, but except for her strong alignment with their abolitionist leanings, she experienced too much of a pull-push relationship with the divine, a sort of war with God, to find comfort there. Her spiritual beliefs aligned more with the progressive views of the Transcendentalists who blossomed around her New England. As with Whitman and Thoreau, Dickinson encountered the divine in nature, and often proffered more questions than answers.

> *Some keep the Sabbath going to Church—*
> *I keep it, staying at Home—*
> *With a Bobolink for a Chorister—*
> *And an Orchard, for a Dome—...*
>
> *God preaches, a noted Clergyman—*
> *And the sermon is never long,*
> *So instead of getting to Heaven, at last—*
> *I'm going, all along.*

But regardless of any philosophical quarrels she might have had with her church, Emily Dickinson embraced their hymnody, and it contributed significantly to her verse. Dickinson's writing has much in common with music even beyond the standard considerations of meter and rhyme. Her distinct punctuation, especially the use of the dash, establishes a definitive, yet often unexpected, cadence; and her use of capitalization emphasizes as an agogic accent would a note of importance within a measure. While many of her poems flow in the meter of her favorite hymns, Dickinson was not afraid to present changing meter or even asymmetry, much in the way that

20th-century composers would feel liberated from the rhythmic and metric confines of the Common Practice Period.

There seems little doubt that as a writer and thinker, Emily Dickinson functioned more as a harbinger of the future than a recipient of success in her lifetime. Misunderstood and unappreciated, she suffered unveiled dismissal because of her gender and eccentricities. After her death at age 55, almost 1,800 poems were discovered and collected. These works resided in a variety of locations and in numerous formats—within her desk on fine stationery, enclosed in her prolific correspondence, and even through her own attempts at self-publication in small booklets of poetry, fascicles constructed from folded paper and handsewn. Her family also found fragments of verse on scraps of paper, discarded envelopes, and even candy wrappers. Having only received an anonymous publication of 10 or less in her lifetime, Emily Dickinson would finally receive a posthumous printing of a complete volume of her verse in 1955, almost 70 years after her death, by Harvard University Press.

When examining her entire oeuvre, there seems something especially provocative and captivating about her opening lines, often the only part I can quote accurately from memory. They circle in my head in a repeating cycle like an earworm does with a musical fragment. Perhaps the fact that she did not title her poems, and thus the first lines undertake a dual purpose, strengthens their impact. Who can deny the arresting cadence and imagery of these opening words? No matter how many times I have read or recited them, they still leap off the page with urgency as if being revealed for the first time.

> *Because I could not stop for Death—/ He kindly stopped*
> *for me—...*
> *My life closed twice before its close—...*
> *Success is counted sweetest/ By those who ne'er succeed...*

I heard a Fly buzz—when I died—...
If you were coming in the Fall,/ I'd brush the Summer by...
I measure every Grief I meet...
A Word dropped careless on a Page...
She sweeps with many-colored Brooms—...
They say that "Time assuages"—/Time never did assuage—...
This is my letter to the World/ That never wrote to Me—...

I am grateful that Emily Dickinson gifted us with such a prolific collection of verse because an "undiscovered" one seems to be waiting for me when I need it. Only recently did I discover "A Word made Flesh is seldom" for the first time. It is one of her poems with an unknown date of creation although some scholars have speculated that it might have been written circa 1862 when many of her poems that celebrate linguistics were conceived.

A Word made Flesh is seldom
And tremblingly partook
Nor then perhaps reported
But have I not mistook
Each one of us has tasted
With ecstasies of stealth
The very food debated
To our specific strength—

A Word that breathes distinctly
Has not the power to die
Cohesive as the Spirit
It may expire if He—
"Made Flesh and dwelt among us"
Could condescension be
Like this consent of Language

This loved Philology.

The lines reveal her usual prowess and veiled, multi-layered meanings. Even experts find this one a bit tricky to excavate and suggest a variety of possible interpretations. What appears certain is that Dickinson took the opening line from The Gospel of John, whose first chapter provides the theological foundation for the Christian faith— Jesus as Word and as God, dwelling among us and in us. John 1:1 declares, "In the beginning was the Word, and the Word was with God, and the Word was God." Then in verse 14, we read the eponymous phrase, "The Word became flesh and dwelt among us." Emily Dickinson rarely used quotation marks, so it is of great importance that she quotes the scripture here. As in other poems, she draws on traditional Christian beliefs, and then reshapes and expands them to reflect her worldview. The poet is not being irreligious, quite the opposite. Emily Dickinson sought common ground between the faith of her childhood and her reverence for the written word. That convergence feels familiar to me.

The poetry of Emily Dickinson illuminates many paths that lead us to the divine. Her forging of verse that exalts nature reflects the work of a Creator God who fashioned the grandest galaxies and also the industrious ant. In the book of Job, God reminds us how much we can learn from nature. "But ask the animals, and they will teach you, or the birds of the air, and they will tell you; ask the plants of the earth, and they will teach you, and the fish of the sea will declare to you." (Job 12:7-8). Jesus, God enfleshed, also pointed to nature as a conduit to divine and faithful living. He taught us to consider the lilies of the field, the mustard seed, and the fig tree. A resourceful teacher, Jesus taught spiritual lessons with the ordinary objects around him—lamps, coins, and jars. Emily Dickinson did the same.

Whatever time of year or season in life, a reader can discover at least one Dickinson poem, and probably more, that speaks to the moment and deepens the reflection of the heart and soul. Her relevance remains, and I believe fulfills her sincerest desire to create timeless words that would keep her ever present.

> *Beauty crowds me till I die*
> *Beauty mercy have on me*
> *But if I expire today*
> *Let it be in sight of thee—*

1The Dickinson poetry quotations in this essay come from Final Harvest: Emily Dickinson's Poems. Selected by Thomas H. Johnson. Little, Brown and Company, 1961.

18

Cana of Galilee by Caroline Liberatore

A feast was wrought one eve in Galilee
Wedding guests reclined to feign their ease

Stale lips edged with grape stains and crumbs
Testify their futile nibbling to pacify and numb

But as they pat their middles and heave deep sighs
Their insides twist with false alibi

Their cravings, even still, are not yet appeased
All their vain snackings have left their souls lean

Then the music sours from gazes askance
So a man of simple stature halts his dance

He considers his hands: tactile, primed for scars
And reaches to graze the pitiful, cracked wine jars

At the feel of his benign touch, a faint whisper rings
From craters which, for all their lives, have only known pangs

For a brief, euphoric moment, collective breath is caught
Heartstrings stretched into infinity are quickly pulled taut

The curtain veiling mercy is sliced with a knife
And then, an exhale of ecstasy, an eruption of life—

19

Broken Vase by Joy Schelzel Manning

This orbed vase of colored glass—
meant for bouquets of flowers,
slipped from fingers numb and cracked
from chill that seeped in joints and marrow,
aching my hand's grasp.

The globe hammered slate floor,
crying out a crash and shatter,
shards skidding kaleidoscope color
scraping ridges over grey stone.
The smack echoes in ears ringing,
reeling over visions smashed,
like these pieces—broken and scattered.

Then light beams fire fragments on the floor,
crimson, gold and blue. A whisper-breeze
blows breath into the fissures jagged;
its swirl catches glass dust,
that spirals to gather in light ray's brush.

The flame pours its stoke into the rubble,
touching points, buffing edges smooth.
Teardrops of gold fill each crevice,
fitting segments and soldering to fuse.

Light paints its glow into ordered colors
sculpting vision of a new design.
My fingers catch fire as they clasp the sight:
Beauty rising from ruins.

20

Baby Swallows by Ryan Keating

Baby summer swallows over my door
bulge with black and blue marble eyes,
bare translucent throats and rippled veins
purple with blood, about to burst
from the brittle mud nest clinging
to the crumbling cornbread stucco
by the sheer will of God frail,
vulnerable, awkward, expecting
to be fed as if they could be

unconcerned with why I feel
exposed and weak when I forgive
people plotting against us
and hope the good for them instead
of choking on resentment—

the cat squared below the cocked eye
of the father bird returning home
with dead bugs for his whiny chicks
and a deeper peace for me.

21

Is It Easier to Grieve If You're A Therapist by Pam Luschei

Some people say what they think. It's not a bad thing. A few months after my husband suddenly died in 2018, a woman asked the unavoidable question; "Does it make it any easier to grieve because you are a therapist?" As I recall, I uttered some benign response, like, "I'm not sure", while simultaneously thinking how insensitive it sounded at the time. However, I'm now able to reflect back and consider the question to be legitimate.

As I've gained clarity and found my footing, I can relate to the question from a different perspective. It would be like if I was teaching a course on oceanography. As the instructor, I would know the types of sea life in the ocean. I would be able to give statistics on the depths of bodies of water. I would recite facts about life below the water relating to each urchin, fish, and marine animal. I could describe in words what lies below the surface from textbooks and pictures. However, my teaching would be limited, if I never put on a wetsuit and scuba gear to go below the water. I only knew what I learned from reading and studying.

The day my husband died I put on a wetsuit, mask, and oxygen tank and took the dive below the surface. I was now in a place where I could fully experience all of what I had learned. With my mask on, I could see, touch, hear, and explore what I know about grief in a way like never before. I was surrounded and fully immersed in my own personal journey of grief.

So the next question to consider is, "how has my personal experience affected my professional work with grieving clients?" As I reflect I've formed some conclusions and observations. When listening to a client share their story I can no longer stand on the shore as a neutral observer. I have a revised and expanded ability to empathize and care. My compassion has deepened and widened. In graduate school therapists are trained to be objective and keep a distance, offering reflection and observation for the client. In other words, professional aloofness.

From my own journey, I now have a greater bandwidth of acceptance and presence to offer clients. I can nod and utter the words, "I know", identifying with them in their pain. I offer the tissue box and say how truly sorry I am for their loss. The therapy office is a sacred space for the client as I welcome them to grieve and honor their loved one.

As someone who has gone to the depths, I am able to be a tour guide and offer hope on the journey. Self-disclosure is a debatable issue as a therapist. Do I tell my client anything about me? How much do I share? When a client comes to the office, it's about them. However, the relationship that I have with them is an important part of the healing process. It's not just information. It's about transformation. I have found that I can tell them my story in a few sentences to help them know there is a way through. Like watching someone climbing out of a ditch, I have to give them a cup of cool water. I was once in the ditch. 2 Corinthians 1:3-5 (NIV) speaks to this truth, "Praise be to the God and Father of our Lord Jesus Christ, the Father of compassion and the God of all comfort, who comforts us in our all troubles so that we can comfort those in any trouble with the comfort we ourselves have received from God. For just as the sufferings of Christ flow over into our lives, so also through Christ our comfort overflows." With this truth, I'm able to give to others what I've been given.

The entire first year following my husband's death I saw a therapist. I sat on the couch, not in the chair. I wept, talked, was listened to, and heard. It was a balm for my grief-stricken soul. My therapist was acquainted with grief. I was grateful she had been where I was. She gave me hope without using words. There's a quote that says, "People don't care how much you know until they know how much you care." I can agree both as a client and a therapist.

So back to the original question the woman posed to me, "does it make it easier to grieve because you're a therapist?" I don't think the word "easier" describes it. Grieving isn't easy. It's excruciatingly hard, extremely painful, growth-producing, faith-building, and transformative. Knowing that it's going to be difficult to climb a mountain, doesn't mean you don't climb it. My mind tells me it's hard. My faith tells me I'm not alone. My spirit tells me I'm weak. My soul tells me it's going to hurt.

Maybe being a therapist allowed me to get the tools I needed sooner. But then, being a person of faith put me in a position of running to the Lord sooner, as well. I knew where to go. It's like knowing where your disaster kit is located before the disaster. You can find what you need when you know where it is. It's quite possible that being a therapist helped me grieve with more intention than if

I wasn't a therapist. What I do know is that grieving has made me a better therapist, allowing me to offer others a way through.

I wasn't a therapist. What I do know is that grieving has made me a better therapist, allowing me to offer others a way through.

22

For Glory and Beauty by Nicole Byrum

Seated in the wooden pew on Sunday morning, I glanced about our small, simple sanctuary. While there's nothing particularly captivating about its appearance, I've come to love the wooden beams and the tall pointed rooftop. I looked upon the solitary piano and the simply constructed pulpit. The simplicity of the room seemed to only enhance the focus on God's glory. And yet, I smiled when my eyes fell on the communion table, always adorned with a seasonal bouquet of flowers.

As the pastor concluded his sermon, it occurred to me that the presence of the flowers had nothing to do with the effectiveness of the message. Had they been absent the truths communicated in the sermon would have been exactly the same. But with them, there existed a beauty that otherwise would not have been.

This thought reminded me of Exodus 28 when Moses received instructions from God concerning the priestly garments of the

Tabernacle. He was given so many details regarding the materials, jewels, and construction of these clothing items! However, my favorite part of the elaborate description is the *why* of it all. Verses 2 and 28 states that these holy garments were for *glory and beauty.*

I remember the first time I read that chapter of the Bible and being blown away by the thought that our God is a lover of beauty —and that beauty serves a distinct purpose. The longer I thought about it, I could only come to this conclusion: *of course, God loves beauty.* Not only did the Creator of the universe create a world that is defined by order and efficiency, but He created it full of beautiful scenery. The sun not only sets, but it sets in a blaze of brilliant colors. Jagged mountains, deep oceans, fields of wheat, starry skies...all proclaim the work of His hands. Even so, it's plausible He saved His most beautiful creation for last when He formed Eve from the rib of Adam.

Because we are human beings made in the Image of God, we desire and are drawn to beauty. While this is true of both men and women, women especially long not only to see beauty but to *be* beauty. Our hearts want to know, *Am I beautiful?* To answer this question we often consult the nearest mirror, evaluating our beauty by the cut and color of our hair, the current smoothness of our complexion, and the way our clothes fit our bodies. Please hear me clearly, I'm not saying that physical beauty is unimportant—on the contrary, I think God has gifted all women greatly in this area. However, the mirror cannot unveil the fullness of beauty given to women, especially of those who are in Christ.

Psalm 139:13-15 tells us that we have been fearfully and wonderfully made, formed in the secret place of our mother's womb. And while the essence of beauty was given to us as women at our conception, there is still a greater beauty that our Creator loves and desires for His daughters. This is the beauty of a gentle and quiet spirit, a spirit which seeks to walk in the way of truth and righteousness

(1 Peter 3:4). Such a spirit is displayed in the woman of Proverbs 31 who clothes herself with strength and dignity and is not afraid of the days to come (v.25). This is the spirit shaped only through abiding in Christ and his Word; the spirit that grows in sanctification, being daily conformed to the image of Christ. This is true beauty and the kind of beauty that greatly pleases the Lord. Truly, as we become more like Christ, our beauty increases all the more.

When we speak a kind, encouraging word to a friend or stranger; when we unashamedly proclaim the goodness of God's love and mercy; when we do yet another load of dishes and fold the never-ending pile of laundry with gratitude in our hearts; when we exercise patience with our kids and demonstrate humility with our spouse; when we trust in the Lord to give us all we need for the coming day: this is beauty on display.

Perhaps even more remarkable, this beauty is not without purpose. Just as a painting points to a painter, and a skyscraper to an architect, so all beauty points to a designer, to someone who has carefully molded and crafted his work. I find this to be true while reading classic pieces of literature. While I may love the story and characters, I cannot help but be even more amazed by the creativity and mind of the author. In the same (and even greater) way, our Christ-like beauty serves to point others to Him so that in all things, He might receive glory and honor.

Only a gracious and sovereign God creates women with beauty —as well as the desire for it—and then through Christ, increases it and gives it a great purpose. Like the flowers on the communion table and the priestly garments, we are for glory and beauty. But be encouraged, sister. Our beauty far outweighs the beauty of flowers and robes, for we have within us that which makes us beautiful beyond compare—the spirit of Christ. And in this, our great God is mightily glorified.

23

✤

The patron saint of lost causes holds a jumble sale
by Nadine Ellsworth-Moran

I pick through bins piled with an assemblage
of supplications, some collapsed on both sides,
bent ribs poking through like torn umbrellas,
some too unspeakable to touch in their utterlessness,

the fragile ones already shattered and sifting in bits
to the bottom. A few seem to be in fair condition,
but the undercarriage has fallen out and only
the husk of it in your hand.

My body hinged over the bin edge,
I keep pushing aside these holy oddments, sneakers
grazing the ground beneath, suspended, upended
with my head low, bowed over this well,

as the walls cave in and I begin to winnow again,
one at a time. Somewhere there is the prayer I left
for rubbish, then realized what I'd done—
call it piety that preys on itself, sees the rags

of worn prayers and pulls at the threadedge
unselvaged place until the thinness of them seems
useless to you, useless to You, and I toss them aside
without looking where they fall. After all, how many

times can I wear these words, wear them out,
masticate them, before they are meaningless
strings of letters straining for one another just to keep
the words intact, until even the Amens leave

dust on my fingers. But now, with perspiration
running down my thighs beneath the stolid sun,
these empty hands, soulwracked—
But now, I want my prayer back.

24

Why chapels should look like converted living rooms
by Nadine Ellsworth-Moran

For months, I slept (though I use the term
loosely) on the dark floral sofa
with its thousand scents and memories,
placed just past the new French doors. Still,
fifteen feet away, you broke

your leg shuffling to the bathroom.
I wasn't swift enough to hook
my arms beneath your tender shoulders,
catch your fall, so we sat on the floor
waiting for the ambulance.

Other times, I woke to see you reaching
from your dreams, hand suspended mid-air—
Adam reaching for God across the Sistine
with yearning in your fingertips.

Some nights you called, *Come,*
pray with me, and I would inch across
the wilderness of your bed, careful not
to jar your balsa wood bones, cradle you
and speak holy words till you fell asleep,

our own Pietà. Later, when anyone said
your name, it was followed by, *your mother*
was a saint. I would let this wash over me,
search for its comfort, pluck it from a branch
and bite deeply from its ripeness, letting
the juices run down my chin.

25

Thin Place, With Hummingbirds by Diane Parrish

We live on a tidal estuary that has been a transportation waterway for centuries. Tucked out of the main channel on the opposite bank from where we live is a thin place, only accessible from the water, and I suspect only thin if one arrives in the quiet of the morning in a silent watercraft. I love this place, but I have not been there for weeks.

Illness, the details of which are too tedious to recount, kept me from the river and the kayak. It also kept me from sleeping or even breathing normally and I must admit, its persistent refusal to let go of me also kept me on the verge of despair. I pep-talked and bright-sided myself almost constantly, but after several weeks of feeling terrible, it was hard even to pretend I believed anything I was saying.

I found some relief from my physical symptoms when I started getting out of bed while it was still dark to sit by the river and breathe the humid air before the sun could turn it into steam. I'd watch the egrets and herons find their morning meal. I'd wave to the fishermen headed out to sea. I'd catch glimpses of nature I never would have seen if I'd been healthy enough to sleep through the night. I was grateful for these blessings, but they were insufficient to heal the sorry state of my spirit.

I might have found solace in my garden near the water. There we always plant salvia "black and bloom", which most years flowers from June until frost and reliably attract a hummingbird or two several times a day. For some reason this summer the plants hadn't bloomed at all, not a single blossom. Maybe the salvia had what I had. I really missed the hummingbirds and hoped they'd find a substitute flower enticing enough to stop by our garden anyway, so I kept looking for them.

After many days of watching with no luck, on one dark morning, not a foot from of my face, the tiniest of hummingbirds whizzed past in a blur, so swift I almost doubted I'd really seen it. But I was thrilled. A second later came another. And another. And another. Thirty, forty hummingbirds, so close I could have touched them, shot by in a line. One after another, all the hummingbirds in the world, or so it seemed, flashed their iridescent wings before my eyes. What nature of miracle was this?

Hummingbirds are creatures of habit who will visit the same flowers and feeders year after year and return to the place they were born to raise their young. But they are also adaptable and will adjust their flight path if the expected food source is not available. Without the salvia's nectar, the birds must have mapped a different route that zipped through our garden without stopping. I returned every morning expecting, hoping, to see the same sight again.

I never did. Not a single bird flew that path again on any of the mornings I waited for them. Eventually, our salvia did flower and attract a hummingbird or two, but the hummingbird superhighway had apparently closed.

Why did all those hummingbirds fly single file across my line of vision that one magical morning? The scientific explanation is that they were hungry and didn't find food where it used to be. But so many? That one and only time? I have another explanation. At a time when I really needed the hope and peace that I would have found in the thin place I couldn't reach, the hummingbirds brought the thin place to me.

26

The Alchemy of Kindness
by Mary Anne Abdo

Kindness is the way to find a raised head with a smile.
Shadowy figures love kindness for it feeds their soul.
Like a friend that goes haunting into that heavenly night.
Amongst the feathers he is now lost to the wind.
People do not notice the nuisances of life.
The skin is a healing encasement.
Like Italian silk scarves with colors of green and gold.
Walking into this feeble connection.
We may stand-alone on this earth.
But we are never really alone by the cypress tree.
Kindness changes misunderstood words.
Into the light of clarity.
We lose and yet remember those dreams.
Those dreams that guide us towards the answers we seek.
Familiar celebrations by the fireplace.

As our children were laughing and playing.
So much kindness.
Leaves will tumble like the sands of time.
Grain by grain.
Leaf by falling leaf beckoning winter's call.
The earth is famous to those who stop and ponder.
Every child chases fireflies.
The simplicity of childhood needs no introduction.
It is just beauty.
Our vegetable and flower gardens were ripe at harvest.
Making bouquets and potluck suppers.
Their fragrance is kindness to all who entered our kitchens.
Wafting through the neighbor's windows.
Dishes are now falling apart.
Someday those shatter pieces will form a beautiful mosaic.
Of kindness in your honor.
Squinting my eyes from that mysterious light.
Stars shine like iridescent orbs.
The golden act of transforming kindness will be etched.
A never fading form of spiritual elegance.

27

Speechless by Kimberly Phinney

I have thought so long,
but I cannot find
a fresh metaphor
or the right words
to say (just so)
what You are
and what I am not.

Like how I fail
and how You do not:
You, like pylons driven
deep into the ground
to sure up the shore.
You, holding earth in place
not matter

the midnight storms,
the beating winds,
the rising tides,
setting me
awash.

Or, how I am so small
and You are not:
You, like the infinite
water's reach
spanning across oceans—
You, baptizing its
granule forms—
to smooth edges
to make pressure
for new life—
birthing a pearl
of great worth.

It's all been said,
I know.
So, I haven't
the right words
for You.
You, who are *The Word*—
the beginning
and the end.
And how I am not.

Or how You are every word
thereafter:
life breathed—

plucked from our thoughts,
bowed down
and speechless
before You.

28

The Song Master's Tale by Chrissy Callahan

What about Aurora?" Jett, the young conductor asked. "How did you train her to be so skilled at her song?"

The Song Master smiled. It was a question often asked by new conductors and a story he was happy to tell.

"Aurora was a cheerful young girl," the Song Master explained. "She was eager to play her song for anyone who would listen."

"So it was years of practice then? She was destined to be skilled from the start?" Jett nodded proudly to himself as he put the pieces together. This conductor business was easier than he thought.

"Not quite." The Song Master's correction interrupted Jett's self-congratulations. "Come, sit. I will tell you her story."

* * *

The Song Master looked Aurora's way. Her song had become unsteady in the wake of recent events. He saw her faltering and tried to steady her. She couldn't seem to focus on him, though.

"Aurora," the Song Master called. "Look at me."

Aurora was becoming frantic. Why couldn't she play her song? The Song Master watched with sorrow as Aurora desperately tried to remember the notes she had practiced from her youth. *"Aurora, look at me."*

The cacklers began to circle Aurora, dancing as they howled their jeers:

> *Oh Aurora!*
> *Look what you've done.*
> *You've missed your step,*
> *And now your tune is gone!*

There was nothing more Aurora could think to do. She stumbled down the way, losing piece by piece of her song as she went.

"That's enough," the Song Master called after the cacklers. He hadn't raised his voice in the slightest, yet his words pierced their hearts.

"Surely you aren't serious," they countered. "Look at her! She has lost her song. Not too much longer and she'll be one of us."

"No," the Song Master replied. "She will sing again."

"Surely he can't be right," the cacklers thought to themselves. Then again, they had never known the Song Master to be wrong.

* * *

"Wait, Aurora lost her song?" Jett interrupted, stunned. "But she sings so beautifully today!"

The Song Master paused and smiled. That was often the reaction of new conductors, yet he never wearied of it. That was how he knew they were beginning to understand.

"Let me ask you something, Jett." The Song Master paused again to ensure he had Jett's full attention. "Who treasures their song more? The one who always had it or the one who lost it yet had it restored to them again?"

"I suppose the one who knows what it's like to be without it," Jett responded sheepishly.

The Song Master smiled. "Now as I was saying..."

* * *

"Aurora! I haven't seen you in a while. Wh-where's your song?" Finally realizing what was so different about Aurora, Peter now looked at her with concern.

"I've lost it, Peter. I looked and looked, I tried to play, but I can't. I fear it's gone for good now. I couldn't play it even if I found it." Aurora could hardly lift her eyes. If only she could go back...

"Oh, don't say that, Aurora. We'll find your song. You know the Song Master will help you." Peter tried reassuring her, but he could see she wasn't convinced.

"How can you know, Peter? The cacklers were right. I messed up—How could I sing it again? Can it even be returned to me while I'm in this state?"

"Don't listen to those cacklers, Aurora. All they want is to get you to stop singing. Come with me. We'll find your song." Peter knew the Song Master would help Aurora, but as he looked at her, he also saw how weak she had become. She wasn't strong enough to learn her song by herself. *Come with me, Aurora. We'll get your song back.*

* * *

"Peter... Not Aurora's Peter? The quiet one?" Jett was becoming more confused with each curveball. Now he was supposed to believe that one of the softest-spoken singers of his district was the one who helped Aurora regain her strength?

"You're surprised?" The Song Master questioned. "Why is that?"

"Oh, it's just, well, nevermind. Please continue." Jett determined to keep his mouth shut for the rest of the story.

* * *

"Come on, Aurora. We're almost there." Peter reassured her. Bethany and Cedric had joined in and were supporting her on each side. Together they pushed past the cacklers, bringing Aurora closer and closer to the Song Master. The Song Master ran to meet them.

"Song Master!" Peter called. "Can you help Aurora find her song?"

Aurora dared not lift her eyes. She could see his feet moving closer and longed for everything to be okay again. Her song was gone, though. Could she face him?

"Aurora," the Song Master said gently, "Aurora, come here so I can teach you your song."

Aurora's eyes shot up. "My song?" She could feel tears welling. "You mean I...I can learn my song again?"

"Aurora, I have a new song for you, and you will sing it well. Will you let me teach you?" The Song Master's voice was kind, and its steadiness drowned out the sound of the cacklers behind her.

The Song Master sat with Aurora and began to teach her the new melody. Aurora couldn't believe it... Could it be that this new song was even more beautiful than the one she lost?

* * *

"Hello, Song Master!" Aurora called out with a smile as she passed him and Jett.

Jett marveled. This woman did not appear as one who had lost her song. No, her face shined and her eyes danced. She seemed to float as she moved.

"Song Master, how can this be?" Jett couldn't help one last question.

The Song Master put his hand on Jett's shoulder. "Jett, I have come to save that which was lost. There are people all over this world longing to be restored, and that mission is what I charge each one of you with now too."

29

White-washed tombs by Brittney Dederman

I walk across this path alone,
barren lands and fallen trees lie before me,
the cracked road outstretched for miles,
and me, a mangled human wanting a purpose.

I stumble across a white tomb,
with golden trims along its roofing,
shiny tiles line the pathway,
and even a statue of an angel tops the palace off.

I've been tired of this life,
walking this broken path alone,
maybe this place of hope has what I seek?

I open the big iron door,

expecting to find something grand,
I instead find nothing but disappointment.

The tomb reeks of death and havoc,
the coffins inside are dusty and moldy,
rats scurry at my feet and cobwebs lines each corner.

This is not a place of hope,
just a similar site with a like-minded person,
but maybe this is where I belong.

Beautiful on the outside but rotting on the inside,
this structure and I are the same.

—why we need a savior

30

Prairie Girl by Kirk Jordan

In Oklahoma, oak trees
keep their leaves
through the stripping winter blast,
even to the time when Red Bud bud.

So, when all the leaves that will fall—fall
into the bags we've placed to catch 'em,
we flee, to a land of wafting umber,
under the wild sky
where light and line and twine emerge
in a surge of tall grass habitat.

Twenty miles west of town,
we round the river bend and then
exit, "S"ing upward
into Prue, through these hills of calico –
Oh! What variety of brown.

Down a copper canyon
Up a chocolate rill,
Allemande left to the Cinnamon hill.
Bow to your partner, kiss her cheek,
Park the car and let wind speak!

The sweep before our eyes is
all staccato, shredded wheat--
chaotic spew,
the stuff of cereal,
Ethereal, with toast

An undulating ocean
made of wooden grass;

The waves go out like weaving rain;
We hear the crash of distant surf --
Or sometimes – with the heavy wind
the sound of padded bamboo clicking,
Everything is moving but
the stalwart rocks
or blackened remnants of hardwood trees, strewn bold
like cracks upon the sky.

The day goes late
with wash of rye, marmalade and gold

And Kerry looks o'r the prairie
her hair wafting back
like these heavenly weeds.

31

Leafless by Jordan Sleed

Do you resent this tree,
No longer bearing leaves
Standing tall, across from one whose continue to grow?

Or do I shortsightedly
Issue such fixated decrees
That *I* forget what *you* must know?

These branches have not given up,
    have not bitterly labored in vain.
No, subtle winds have carried all their losses
    to needful, empty plains.

And I suppose the evergreen
    will be unto me shade,
As I recall—leafless trees
    are resurrections displayed.

32

This Apron by Caitlin N. Pate

This apron—
Dusted, smudged, and stained—
tells a beautiful story,
A woven tapestry
Of a life lived simply,
Happily.

It recalls nervous hands
Wiping flour and bits of dough off as she ran to greet
Her love with a kiss;
As well as kneeling in the fresh spring dirt,
sowing tiny seeds
In hope of harvest.

It remembers catching
Tears of little ones,
Overwhelmed and in need of comfort;
And receiving
still-warm eggs,
Carefully cradled into its folds to be carried
Into the kitchen.

It will never forget
The purple stains
of summer's first blackberries,
Gathered and eaten
In the sunshine;
Nor how family, home, and hope
Were tied together
By its apron strings.

33

Repentance by Hannah Nelson

I feel the ache inside my chest,
The pulsing pain, it steals my breath.
How could this have happened? Is this real life?
Where are you, God? Thought you were on my side.

I know I shouldn't question you,
But tell me what am I to do?
I just can't wrap my mind around all this,
Didn't I serve you and give my best?

I want to feel you close by my side,
But part of me wants to run and hide.
Do I put on the mask, act like I'm fine?
Do I dare admit what I feel inside?

Just like I learned from Adam and Eve,
Try to cover my shame with fig leaves,
I know I've let You down, messed up again,
I'm hurting and I know I can't pretend.

Like the gushing red blood from a wound,
Like the stem falling as it is pruned,
This broken confession spills from my lips,
"God, I don't know how to trust you with this."

Like the man whose son had a demon,
Who brought him to Jesus to heal him,
My heart cries out for your help to believe,
"I believe, but Lord, help my unbelief!"

Then like the shining light peaking out
From behind the thickest, dark storm clouds,
Your forgiveness and peace eclipse my soul,
Your grace consumes my pain; You make me whole.

You don't want me to strive on my own,
You call this prodigal to run home.
You embrace me along with all my mess,
You take the weight of my sin on yourself,
You welcome my questions and brokenness,
And You call me Chosen and name me Blessed.

34

The Great Green Picnic Table by Leslie Bustard

I have had, through the years, a picture in my mind's eye of the perfect outdoor wooden table, set with white table linens, tall candles in silver holders, vintage blue chintz plates, and shining silverware. Twinkling lights are strung above, with white peonies placed in the correct spots as to not block anyone's view. It is at once classic and rustic and very inviting for a gathering of twenty or so friends. My Tumblr page will attest to this vision, as variations of this theme have been posted often.

My back patio, though, does not feature my dream outdoor table. It holds a generic green, heavy-duty plastic, one-piece picnic table. Let me repeat what I have owned for seventeen years... *a generic green, heavy-duty plastic, one-piece picnic table.*

One summer, seventeen years ago, Ned and I used a Costco membership in order to buy the same picnic table that our neighbors had just placed in their backyard. Our children were young, and we knew we needed something sturdy and in our price range. This particular table could sit lots of wiggly little bodies, take all the stickiness of melted popsicles, and not be stained by the colors of outdoor crafts. It could also seat a family of five and any friends we may want joining us for a meal. An added bonus—it could double as a fort or hiding place. Although I really would have liked something lovely to look at, such as the ones featured in magazines, I went with practical.

Over the past several decades, acquiring the right dining room table, kitchen table, or outdoor table has been like the quest for the Holy Grail. Maybe I have desired the right tables because my attention has been drawn so often to how tables, gathered-together people, and food are interwoven throughout Scripture, especially those accounts of Jesus feasting or sharing meals with others.

One of the Gospel stories that never grows old for me is the record of Jesus walking on the road to Emmaus with Cleopas and another disciple. I love how this recollection of Easter Sunday continues on to a house and a table. It then culminates with the three of them sitting around that table breaking bread together. And it's in the breaking of the bread, while they are gathered together *at the table*, that Jesus reveals himself to them as their resurrected Lord.

Gathering family and friends around a table—and many times around my generic green, heavy-duty plastic one-piece picnic table —has been one of the most heart-satisfying ways to show how much I want people to be known and to be loved. It has been a small way to image Jesus in my everyday life. As Andi Ashworth in *Real Love for Real Life: The Art and Work of Caregiving* shares, "Christ has welcomed us into his presence and his kingdom, and we are to imitate him as we welcome others."

Elaborating on the importance of gathering around a table, Andi says,

> "Shared meals around a common table have many wonderful outcomes beyond simply nourishing the body. They create time for relational bonding through conversation, laughter, and listening to each other's stories. They provide a setting where the deeper needs of our souls—aesthetic enjoyment, comfort, feeling of belonging, and a sense of security that comes from being cared for—are tended to."

Early this May, my green picnic table came out of winter storage for yet another summer. The original hardware lost somewhere in the basement, it is now held together by miscellaneous bolts. New this spring is the little puddle that collects in the middle of the table when it rains. Although I do "window-shop" each spring at Costco for a new table, I still haven't found something to replace it. I don't really want to spend the money, and, to my own surprise, I'm not quite ready to get rid of it.

"A Liturgy of Feasting with Friends" from *Every Moment Holy* applies, even to this green table with the water-collecting dip in the middle:

> "But the joy of fellowship and the welcome
> and comfort of friends new and old,
> and the celebration of these blessings of
> food and drink and conversation and laughter
> are the true evidences of things eternal,
> and are the first fruits of that great glad joy
> that is to come and that will be unending."

Around this table....

Around this table, June and July birthday parties have been celebrated, always with special friends and usually including some form of chocolate.

Around this table, friends have lingered late into the night, with the only light being from the bulbs strung along the fence and the various sizes of citronella candles placed between us.

Around this table, out-of-town guests have come for 4th of July and enjoyed grilled hamburgers and hotdogs, coleslaw, and potato salad. They have stayed long enough to run around the back-yard, holding sparklers in their hands and blazing patterns in the darkness.

Around this table, teenagers have hung out, eating pizza and chips, drinking soda, and playing card games.

And around this table, church friends have gathered to eat dinner. Eight people can squeeze around it—three on each side and one on each end. (If young children have come, I will place a picnic blanket on the grass, so that they can eat and run around easily.) My colorful and only-for-summer-and-outdoor-eating plastic plates are used. And for these gatherings, I'll serve a simple main dish, usually something that pairs well with locally grown corn-on-the-cob, hearty bread, and summer berry jam. For dessert, sliced ripe red strawberries topped with homemade whipped cream and mini-chocolate chips will be dished out for everyone.

I still desire to fulfill my vision of the long, wooden table, set in white linens and blue chintz, with the perfect food and wine, lights and flowers—a gathering rich with feasting, talking, and laughing. Those photos I have collected on Tumblr are still playing around in my mind.

But the stories I have collected of family and friends around my great green, heavy-duty plastic, one-piece picnic table do make my heart glad. I have tasted, if only a little, of our New-Creation future, as Isaiah declares "On this mountain, the Lord Almighty will prepare a feast of rich food for the people, a banquet of aged wine—the best of meats and the finest of wines." (Isaiah 25:6) This is where my hope rests—the unending joy of being with all God's people around the table where Jesus welcomes us.

35

Joseph and Julia by Caitlin Deems

Joseph left the Navy and took a job in south Georgia. This is where he met Julia. They crossed paths several times before their eyes actually met. She knew he wasn't from around here. He thought she was perfect. He noticed how each small child and every stooped gentleman paused to greet "Miss Julia." That's how Joseph learned her name. One day he found himself beside her at the counter.

"Hello, Miss Julia."

His eyes spoke more than his words, and she couldn't look away. Each day held the anticipation of seeing her beautiful face and his playful grin. Julia realized that she belonged with Joseph. There were many reasons her parents rejected the idea: he was ten years older, and his skills—farming and electronics—were useless in a mining town still lit by kerosene. They had kept their family together through war and sickness, only to be threatened by a man with a mind as adventurous as their daughter's.

So they gave her a desperate ultimatum: if she left with him, she could never return.

The words echoed in her mind as she looked up at Joseph, in a wagon bound for Florida. He looked at her with the same smiling eyes she had been intrigued by that first day. She dared not look back and she was afraid to look ahead, so she kept her eyes on Joseph. And she remembered...

Each time they met in the store they shared something new.

"I'm Joseph. Joseph Steele."

That name played in her head until the next time they met.

"I want to be a teacher."

This wasn't surprising. He had watched her do sums and help children—and adults—read labels in the store.

"I'd like to work in radio one day. I'm trained for it, I just need some pay right now."

This wasn't surprising. His mind always seemed far away from their little town.

In time, she learned about his home and why he left. He learned that she loved children and had more questions than answers. It went unnoticed, except to the shop owner who overhead these momentary meetings. He secretly hoped something would come of it—the little girl with the heart of gold and the man with the hand-shake you could take to the bank. He smiled the day he overheard Joseph's confession.

"I guess it's my turn..."

He paused, nodding his head in thought.

"I love you."

The shop owner glanced at Julia, who couldn't breathe beneath Joseph's steady eyes. With flushed cheeks she fled, leaving her supplies behind. Joseph grinned with understanding.

"Just put it on my tab, Bill."

"No problem, Joseph. I'll have it delivered directly."

"Thanks, sir. I'll be seeing you."

"Yep, I'll be here."

The next day Julia returned to apologize and to pay his delivery boy.

"It's already covered, Miss Julia."

"Oh please, I'd like to reimburse you. You see…"

"Mr. Steele's taken care of it, ma'am."

She blushed again and her eyes dropped in embarrassment.

"I see," she said timidly.

"He's a good man, Mr. Steele is," the shop owner offered with encouraging eyes.

This gave her just enough courage to smile at the thought of Joseph's kindness.

"I see," she said again.

The next time they met neither could remember what they had come for. Joseph had more confidence in Julia than she had in herself. But the sight of his steady eyes and her newfound respect for his character calmed her spirit as she stood to face him for the first time.

"First, I'd like to thank you. For covering my expenses and having it delivered. And then, well, I love you too, Joseph."

Every monotonous hour spent in that small town was worth it just to hear those words. He smiled, and she answered with a laugh.

"Well then. If it's alright with you, Miss Julia, I'd like to keep covering your expenses, preferably forever. If that's ok."

Tears filled her eyes and joy filled her heart.

"That'd be fine, Joseph."

He gently touched her cheek with his rough hand. Then she led him home to ask her parents' blessing. The shop owner inadvertently let out a holler that made the unsuspecting ladies by the flour jump.

It's best not to attempt to narrate the depth of injury sustained by Julia's young heart at her father's words—if such feelings could be narrated with any accuracy at all. Her mother's angry tears seemed to be bottled up and stored inside of Julia for the rest of her life. Joseph left as he was ordered, but not before whispering to Julia, "This don't change anything for me, but you should take a minute. I'll be at the store tomorrow. If you don't show, I'll understand."

He walked home, praying she would show. She prayed also. She remembered that the word "cleave" means both to cut apart *and* to join together. She now understood how one word had opposite meanings. At eighteen, she could hope to find another man who loved her like Joseph did, or go with the man who had taught her more about God's love for her than any Sunday School lesson ever had.

She decided to go with Joseph and forgive her family. She asked God to either change her mind, or give her perfect peace before morning.

She awoke with perfect peace, kissed them goodbye, and left with her possessions wrapped in linen. Her body felt weak, but the sight of Joseph in his wagon, just like he said, gave her the strength to climb up beside him. Joseph could have shouted from the rooftops, but he respected the trial Julia was enduring. So, he cried a single tear of joy while a sorrowful tear stained her pale blue dress. He lifted her face and the look in his eyes said what words couldn't, comforting her in the only way she could be. She smiled as he kissed her forehead, took up the reins, and headed for the courthouse.

36

Letting Go, Holding On by Hannah Grace M. Staton

The secret lies in letting go. The secret to what, you ask? The secret to the life that is filled with God's joy and peace and all we need. Because letting go lies at the heart of surrender, which forms part of the core of our relationship with God.

Letting Go

Show me what it means to let go,
Because I only want to know
The life that You have planned for me;
Because I only want to go
Deeper into Your love for me;
Because I only want to show
The world a glimpse of You in me.

Letting go means giving up, releasing, setting free, and laying down. The very phrase *letting go* has a graceful ring, and that's just what it is—an act of grace. Without God's grace, we would stubbornly hold on to things we should let go of, refusing to give them up. His grace is shown in our letting go.

Even waiting can be a form of letting go. It may seem like nothing is happening while we are waiting on the Lord, but in reality, we are letting go and surrendering to God's plan. As Ann Voskamp writes, "Waiting is the patience of the long-suffering of letting go. Letting go of the plan, the dream, the map, the vision. Letting the ground of things, the things that you made your ground, letting them give way. Waiting is a letting go to let something grow."

I surrender all that I am
To You, oh God; now take me by the hand
And help me to see
All that You have for me.

Why *letting* go? Because surrendering is an ongoing process. Yes, we yield control of our lives to God at the moment of our conversion, but we must keep doing so every moment afterward. So often we lay something down before God and then pick it back up again. We have to keep taking those things and placing them back where they belong: in God's hands. For only He can hold it all.

I'm letting go
Of the things that cling so close;
I'm casting aside
The barriers that block my view;
I'm laying down my pride
And giving up all to You.
Now take my life and make it new.

We all have something (or many things) we need to let go of, whether it be stubborn pride or lies we hide, a desire to be in control or an illusion of perfection, past hurt or present grudges, or a myriad of other things. Whatever it is that's holding you back, ask God to show you and help you let go.

I come with an offering so small;
Is it really a sacrifice at all?
Yet You who sees when the sparrow falls
Surely rejoice at the slightest break in the wall
That stone-cold encloses my heart.
Only Your love can break it apart.

Letting go has to start where you are. You might not be at the point of having to let go of something major, but that doesn't mean you can't start letting go of smaller things, and it doesn't mean that letting go of those smaller things doesn't matter. Vaneetha Rendall Risner muses, "Letting go is never easy. But maybe in letting go of the smaller things. . .I'm practicing letting go of bigger things. Maybe in the smaller losses, God is preparing me for what only he knows is coming."

Sometimes, Father, I find it hard
To let go—when the broken shards
Of relinquished things cut so sharp,
And I'm left standing with empty hands,
And the weight of the pain, like so much sand,
Piles up deep and wide.
Only You can heal the hurt inside,
My sovereign Protector and my Guide.

Surrender isn't easy. So often we want to hold onto things, even when we know they're hurting us, because we simply can't stand the thought of giving up control. As Rich Mullins sings in *Hold Me Jesus*, "Surrender don't come natural to me / I'd rather fight You for something I don't really want / Than to take what You give that I need / And I've beat my head against so many walls / I'm falling down, I'm falling on my knees."

I can think of a couple of ways this works in our lives. One is when we hold onto something good too tightly, turning it into an idol. In such situations, God sometimes has to gently pry the thing we've idolized out of our hands for a time.

Other times things are hard to let go of, not because they are good, but because the hurt they have caused is deep. Things like regret, guilt, shame, and bitterness can cast sticky tentacles into our hearts that are hard to release—but release them we must if we want to enter into the fullness of the life God has for us.

In letting go,
I find You close.
I catch a glimpse of who You are
And feel the beating of Your heart.
For who but You has given all
To save a world under sin's dark pall?
Who but You knows what full surrender means?
Who but You knows how hard it can be
To yield control and simply lean
On the hope of a joy as yet unseen?

When we let go, we find freedom as we are no longer bound by what held us back. We find peace and hope and joy. Letting go opens the door and lets God's light shine in.

In letting go, we take hold of God, the one who gave up all to win us as His bride, for His own glory and for our good.

Holding On

The sweetness of surrender is giving up lies
And finding hope in what is true;
Facing the death of what I prize
And being given life anew;
Willingly, joyfully losing my life
Only to find it in You.

God doesn't call us to let go of something without offering us something else to hold on to in its place. So we lay down pride and take up humility. We cast off lies and pick up the truth. We relinquish our desire to be in control and place our trust in the One who is already in control. We take off the illusion of perfection and put on Christ's robe of righteousness. We release hurt and hold on to healing. We renounce unjust judgment and choose grace. We get rid of grudges and cling to forgiveness. We stop striving to please others and start seeking to please God above all else.

Often there is a pain in letting go. Yet there is peace within the pain. Our surrender is never in vain. Letting go makes room for God to move.

In surrendering and letting go,
I'm yielding to the mighty flow
Of Your Spirit moving all around,
Yearning to drench this thirsty ground
With newfound joy and hope and peace,
Beautiful fruits of soul release.

Both letting go and holding on involve surrender. Letting go is the surrendering *of* something or someone; holding on is surrendering *to* something or someone. Holding on means that we choose to cling to, rely on, and rest in whatever we deem worthy of our trust. There are so many things we should hold on to—truth, love, peace, joy, and hope among them—but above all, God wants us to hold on to Him. "My soul clings to you; your right hand upholds me" (Psalm 63:8 ESV).

You tell me that the choice is mine
To dwell in shades of darkest night
With hands clenched closed hard and tight
Or with open hands lifted high,
Bathed in the warmth of heaven's light.
So dim my view, so short my sight
That often I do not choose the right.
But still I know that this is true:
Wherever I am, I'm held by You.

One dimension of holding on that is different from letting go is this: as we hold on, we are being held. Even when we don't hold on to God as tightly as we should, He holds on to us. How wonderful it is to be held by the One who never lets go.

37

Kept by Charissa Sylvia

Today was the sort of day forgiveness is made for.

Full of visits to ordinary, tired places
while frustration and apologies
felt locked in perpetual rounds
of impatience. Of worry.

Now the light is falling fast,
as short as I fell every hour and as the sound
of showers and dinner and chores
fill the apartment what's filling my heart is this:

I am kept. So are you.

Kept in clasped hands by mercy
that is spent in full every day
only to rise resurrected at dawn.

Kept in life that knows no limitations -
that isn't less on weary days
because it's not on me to source or sustain.

Today I wasn't a poet,
but, by God, together,
somehow, we were a poem.

38

Lamb on A Ledge by Alexis Ragan

"Behold, I, I myself will search for my sheep." Ezekiel 36:11

There is such a thing as lost ones.

An unkept farm that stood
at the edge of a forgotten sea
made real this plateau
when it became known as
the place wandering sheep go.

Until one dusk ushered in the lullaby of redemption.

A lamb, poor in sight,
broke away from
the hopeless herd and
 took the blind path home.

Roaming deep into night,
bracing winds that bite,
 wet pasture makes for
slippery hooves after eventide.

Flocks tend to float away when destinations are frayed.

She remembered this
facing the unstable rockface,
even saw herself plunging
into the fate-less waves.

Tossed against death hill,
feet frozen and cast down,
no way to hush the beat
of her wool-soft soul —
sliding, she inched off the cold cliff
into heartless end —

Until the babe, bleating, glanced up
to see the silhouette of a staff
and eyes that spoke of home —

Was this the owner she heard looks for the lost all along?

He took firm hold of the hoof with
his right hand and carried her
where the rest of the rescued flow.

Since then, the ranch,
whose reputation has been reversed
to one with redemptive tendencies,
can never cease to speak of when
The Shepherd saves
a lamb on a ledge.

39

natal joy by Sarah L. Frantz

You slip into warm hands
With a rush and a groan

Held and examined
Vernix laden bundle

Advent waiting
Your birth and His

Small, round head...body
Wrapped in warmed towel

We witness, we wait, we see

And as the pulsing stops, scissors snip you loose and

I've been holding my breath without even knowing it

<h1 style="text-align:center">40</h1>

Jehovah Shammah by J.D. Isip

Was it you, O Lord, who lifted this lifeless self
    to breathe-in your world
    to tremble before wind and icy days
    to drink and to drink too much
    to remember and to cry,
And did You know the clay would come to this
        in a bar somewhere, alone?

Was it You, my God, who called to black velvet shapes
    to cradle heaven and her constellations
      who called to burning mountains
    to release shadow-black birds like arrows aimed at the sun
      who called to the beasts of the field
    to bow before these lower, less noble forms
      who take their fill and scurry away...

And did You think the clay might come to this
                on a street somewhere, alone?

Was it You, O Creator, who shaped man's soul
        to hunger for self and to thirst for sin
                who placed on men eyes
        to long for flesh and to worship it
                who gave man a will
        to be constant as rain, loyal as Luck
                who put in men minds
        to crack and spill and hold nothing...
And could You guess the clay would be this
                in a bed somewhere, alone?

Was it You, O Lord, who came to this lifeless place
        to breathe-in Yourself
        to tremble before doubt and icy faith
        to love and to love too much
        to remember and to cry?
Yet, You knew the clay would come to this
                in a garden somewhere, alone.

41

Mourning and Celebrating Dreams by Linnea Orians

There are dreams, once chased after, that I haven't stepped towards in years. Through distraction, defeat, or replacement, these dreams have somehow landed in the past. It seems neglectful to leave them behind to pursue new desires. As I try to hold both old and new, it becomes increasingly difficult to reconcile them. Yet with every moment I spend with God, he is graciously revealing to me that there is goodness in laying down past dreams. He journeys alongside us as we mourn dreams which have passed us by and celebrate as we embrace new dreams–sovereign over the intricacy of it all.

There is a verse that David wrote in Psalm 37 which I continually return to when attempting to understand desires and dreams: "Delight yourself in the Lord, and he will give you the desires of your heart" (Psalm 37:4, ESV). At a quick read, this appears to be a promise that all of our desires will be fulfilled as long as they are good.

The verse, instead, calls us to know the Lord to the extent which we can't help but marvel in who he is—that we take delight in him—and as an outpouring of that, our hearts will yearn for what the Lord yearns for. In other words, he will give us what *to* desire. This verse is part of the grander plea David is making for God's people to walk closely with the Lord:

> Trust in the Lord, and do good;
>> dwell in the land and befriend faithfulness.
>
> Delight yourself in the Lord,
>> and he will give you the desires of your heart.
>
> Commit your way to the Lord;
>> trust in him, and he will act.
>
> He will bring forth your righteousness as the light,
>> and your justice as the noonday. (Psalm 37:3-6)

Taking David's plea to heart—spending more time with God—another layer of this verse unfolds. While the Lord's goodness does not change, the way we are called to serve the Lord in alignment with his goodness can change (Hebrews 13:8). The dreams and desires I had in high school to serve the Lord look drastically different than the ones I hold today. For years, I thought the desires I had in the past must remain for the rest of my life; if they did not come to pass as I thought the Lord had told me, then it was not okay to move forward. Yet, as we transform to look more and more like Christ, our desires will too.

During high school, my mind was on the path to be an international missionary. The idea turned my heart and consumed my steps. It seemed evident that God was working and that there was a path being forged. As time passed, those same pathways began to close off with logistical problems and resistance from those close to me. In this process, I also realized my desires were shifting and expanding. The dream to be a missionary soon became a desire tucked away in the back of my mind.

That dream now conflicts with my current desires which makes my heart turn. How can this be possible if both desires are placed by God—surely he would not place dreams which are contrary to one another. Before these new dreams take flight, I want to reconcile the old. It leads my mind to wander and wonder: Could it be possible that I failed and these new dreams are the outcome, are they second place to the original dreams?

These fearful thoughts are counter to David's plea…"Commit your way to the Lord; trust in him, and he will act" (vs. 5). God knows my path far better than I do and is sovereign even when I take steps off his path. He is consistently acting on my behalf and on the behalf of his desires for me. That trust in God's sovereignty is where we can find our rest.

Another part of overcoming these fears has been to acknowledge that there is time to mourn. Mourning enables me to acknowledge the dreams I had and that it is okay to lay them down. It makes way for the next season of dreams God is stewarding. Mourning is admitting that I didn't achieve what I thought I would and acknowledging what has come to pass. Mourning is recognizing that I don't know everything but I know God is sovereign. Not only is God's word living and active (Hebrews 4:12), but His desire for our lives is too. All of that enables me to trust that God grew those desires for a time and a purpose and he dimmed them with the same amount of care.

I can rest by knowing that my past desires have led me to where I am meant to be. Perhaps one day, I will be a missionary far away while raising small kids and writing a novel. God can do that. Yet, maybe it will continue to parallel in ways I did not see coming. The desire to reach people far away has translated into loving my neighbor who does not know the gospel and my coworker who needs someone bold enough to tell them the truth. My dream to become a mother came after years of being fearful of raising children. Dreams to write came from realizing I enjoyed writing devotionals for short-term trips and church ministries. God's goodness is present throughout. In all of it, he is placing desires on my heart as I draw nearer and nearer to him—desires far better than I could have dreamt of on my own.

I suspect my dreams will transform again. I hope they do. As God continues to work in me, I pray my desires change to match his. May I commit my ways to the Lord and live with open hands to his plans. So I pray, Lord, give me the desires of my heart.

42

Teach Us to Number Our Days by Ashley C. Shannon

"Can we go to the baby tree?" my daughter asks, her gloved hand in mine.

"Sure," I respond. We keep our steps straight as we head toward the large oak whose branches shade the section of the cemetery once used for infants and young children. I say "once" because this is an older part of the cemetery. Most of the headstones are from the 1930s and 40s.

It is the spring of the year, and the tree buds greet us. We veer around the graves when we arrive, careful not to trample the emerging grass. My daughter, not yet a reader, points to the names on the stones and asks me to read them.

Baby Louie. Baby Nicolai. Pearl. Charles. Skipper. Our Darling Norma.

The one that gets me is a small, smooth stone. Unlike the others, the stone stands tall. The epitaph reads, "Gon [*sic*] But Not Forgotten." The stone tells us that she was seven years old when she died in 1932. Although 90 years have passed, there are flowers at her grave. I puzzle. *Who decorates her grave?* Surely not her parents. They would have been long gone, too—buried somewhere in the yard. Most likely, it is a relative. Perhaps this little girl's life and death are part of family lore. Grief passed on.

It reminds me of a grave plot not far from this one—a cemetery next to a Nebraska cornfield. It marks the grave of my great-great uncle. He was born in 1878 and buried in 1887, making him nine years old. Just like the decorated tomb under the baby tree, I wonder about the story of my great-great uncle—a story that wasn't passed on.

We have no family at the cemetery with the baby tree, but we often visit because it is a short walk from our home. We also see neighbors here. They come to walk or run. It is quiet. The hills roll on and on with mature trees dotting the sections. We have never walked the whole space, but it goes for acres. It is the biggest in town.

After we visit the baby tree, my daughter points us toward the statue of a woman draped in a long dress and hood. I know to expect her, but her life-like presence startles me. She looks out at the vast headstones. Mourners have placed broken watches, quarters, and bells on the armrest near her hands. My daughter says she looks royal as she sits on her throne, scrutinizing all who pass. Her face is not gentle, as a statue in a graveyard might be, but her solemn expression shows power. I imagine she also holds anger as she accepts the broken clocks.

Once, when we lived in South Carolina, my friend and I, along with our combined five children, went to a forgotten graveyard. It held the remains of a church built after the Revolutionary War. Two interior brick walls remained, but the church lacked a roof or front door. Since it was fall in the coastal South, our children wore sweatshirts with shorts and sandals. They played near the ruins as my friend and I wandered the yard. We read the names and dates of the residents. Then we crouched to read a gravestone that lay horizontally. It was broken into five large pieces. Over the past 200 years, the wind and rain have worn the stone, but we read the letters with a little rub of dirt. The epitaph said, "An eminent physician and courtly gentleman," and said that the stone was placed by his widow. Unlike memorial stones today, it was wordy but poetic.

That afternoon, while my children napped in their rooms, I posted the picture of our morning at the South Carolina cemetery to social media. In the picture was another broken headstone, this one vertical. The sunshine streamed down on it as brown leaves nestled its base. In the distance, our children played. I wrote, "Encountered this today. It puts everything in perspective. What are you living for? Will it matter 100 years from now? May we invest our time and resources in the things that matter and last."

As my kids grow and change, I wonder how to invest well. With every birthday, I fight time. I scroll through my phone's photo log to see baby photos and toddler videos. These living memories no longer represent our reality. In their place are big kids who go to school and tell me things like, "Mom, I'll make fruit salad for dinner tonight," and "Mom, we really need to buy more fruit. It's just not healthy eating only apples."

Part of me wants to jump back to the years of middle-of-the-night rockings and daily cleanings of splattered sauce on the walls. When full cheeks stared up at me, and clumsy tongues said my practiced name. A time when tears and giggles came within minutes of each other. But the cemetery reminds me there is no way back. There is only forward.

In the psalm attributed to Moses, it says, "Teach us to number our days, that we may gain a heart of wisdom." (Psalm 90:12) Loss and grief have a unique way of reshaping our hearts. I have never visited a grave that held my child or spouse, but I have had friends and family touched by this grief. And this marching on of time, although different than a loss of a loved one, hints at its own type of sorrow.

How do we move on?

My daughter and I turn to walk back to our neighborhood. We leave the baby tree and the woman draped in robes. The best way I know how to honor the families of the children at the baby tree is to treasure this moment. My daughter's blonde hair wisps out from under her winter cap, and her coat swishes as we walk down the hill to the trodden path that will take us home. As the sun comes from behind the clouds, my daughter tells me her spring birthday plans and party wishes. I listen.

Soon the flowers will burst up from their dormant winter sleep. Already the robins are returning. Our house will celebrate birthdays, then the summer heat will beckon us to eat watermelon for dinner and swim until our fingers are prunes. Time will continue to carry on. But today—now—I invest in our walk home and trust it will make a difference 100 years from now.

43

The Shadow: Walking Through Grief by Liz Trujillo

I'm not a fan of dark shadows at night.

Whether walking downtown or even in my own neighborhood, I will stay closer to the light so I can see where I'm going. Partly because I have depth perception issues now that I'm in my 40's, but mostly because I just don't like dark shadows.

The only time I really enjoy the dark is when I'm all cuddled up on the couch watching a movie or my favorite binge-worthy show, "Downton Abbey". The lights can be turned way down low to help me drift away into the storyline or just drift off to sleep. It's a shadow of my own choosing; the shadow I can handle at home with the lights down low.

But sometimes, we aren't even looking for the shadows—they just find us.

The shadow that comes with the death of a loved one can often feel like it follows us everywhere. Grief lingers and its shadow stretches into every facet of our lives, from the moment we wake up till our head hits the uncomfortable pillows at night—the ache of losing someone and the immense grief that follows can feel like a dark shadow creeping up behind us.

Grief is hard and it hurts. I can tell you firsthand that the loss of my father impacted my everyday life as no other event has before. In good and in hard ways, this grief journey has taught me some very important lessons. Mainly, I've learned (and continue to learn) that grief is not a 'one and done' emotion, but rather a series of steps on a journey. As painful as it is when the darkness and heaviness of grief creep in unexpectedly, there is also this hope we can cling to:

God promises to be *with* us.

We've just celebrated the Christmas season and I love observing Advent with friends and family alike. The beauty and great anticipation of Advent is the arrival of The Messiah—Jesus, God *With* Us. Long ago, the nation of Israel had been expecting The Messiah to come and set them free, desperately longing for rescue and redemption. Now here we are all these years later, in the anticipation of the next Advent, waiting for Jesus to return and make all things right.

In the middle of the shadow of death

In the waiting and longing for light and hope to break through,

In the chaos that comes when we can't see things clearly,

We can look at God's Word and remember that He makes good on His promises to be with us, to be near to the brokenhearted, and to be present in our pain.

We see in God's Word that Zechariah burst into a song of praise after the birth of his son John The Baptist, declaring:

"Because of our God's merciful compassion,
the dawn from on high will visit us
to shine on those who live in darkness

and the shadow of death,

to guide our feet into the way of peace. (Luke 1:78-79)

God knew that His children way back then would need a guide through loss and pain. He understood that grief wasn't just a journey for travelers of times past but also for you and for me. It's a road that we will all walk, but it isn't the destination where we will dwell. We get to have the warmth of His light guiding us into peace. And if He sent Jesus to lead us into peace, He is simultaneously leading us out of the shadows and into His light, back to the land of the living.

The Psalmist reflects and sings a song as well:

"Yea, though I walk through the valley of the shadow of death,

I will fear no evil;

For You are with me;

Your rod and Your staff, they comfort me." (Psalm 23: 4)

The journey of loss and grief is a walk-through, not a walk-to. On this journey, we have the company of our compassionate Lord, Immanuel, God With Us. His rod corrects our vision in the dark nights of our soul and His staff guides our way and helps us course correct to keep us safely in His care.

Again, in the Psalms David recalls the promise of The Lord's presence in his deepest and darkest valleys:

"Where can I go from your Spirit?

Where can I flee from your presence?

If I go up to the heavens, you are there;

if I make my bed in the depths, you are there.

If I rise on the wings of the dawn,

if I settle on the far side of the sea,

even there your hand will guide me,

your right hand will hold me fast.

If I say, "Surely the darkness will hide me

and the light become night around me,"

even the darkness will not be dark to you;
the night will shine like the day,
for darkness is as light to you." (Psalm 139: 7-12)

Even our present darkness will not be dark to Our Lord.

Even our deepest valleys of pain are no match for His promised presence.

He is God With Us.

In the happy times and in the heartache,

In the highest and most celebratory times in life and in the empty house after loved ones have gone on to eternity,

In the depths of desperation, we can be sure He is with us.

In the attempts to escape His loving grip on us and in the remembrance that we don't need to fight Him off, He is with us.

In this new year, may we remember that where there are shadows, there is proof of light.

The Dawn From On High for those experiencing dark shadows,

The Bright And Morning Star for those mourning and grieving,

The Prince of Peace for those in pain,

The Wonderful Counselor for those needing to pour out their hearts before Him,

The Mighty God for those who feel so weak,

The Everlasting Father for those needing to reach out to Him to be lifted up.

He is God with us—even in the valley of the shadow of death.

And He will lead us all into the way of peace.

44

This is the Day the Lord
Has Made by Ashlee Spear

Your feet find the floor, and you hear yourself say:
This is the day the Lord has made.
Blinds split apart now, in bounds the sun,
relentless and pure as a golden retriever.
The day is worth rising for, yes, and
I'll rejoice and be glad in it.

The night, the hours spent stiff in the grip
of dreamless, restless sleeplessness,
the tick of the clock's taunting tick toward dawn—
shudder once, and leave it. Instead recall
how all through the night, a Voice told a body:
I will stay with you.

Now here on your nightstand, carefully stacked
are pages of rainbows drawn by your child,
the fruit-scented marker still fresh on the paper.
More are taped up, scattered around.
Scraps of joy that are new, and yours to find.
The day is brimming and you step into it, half-alive.

Half-sentences, half-thoughts on their way to birth,
will bubble and sputter, dissolve or burst
or run down the drain all day today, still
This is the day the Lord has made.
These are the words your mind will repeat:
I will rejoice and be glad in it.

45

Personality by Peter Lilly

'I know of no other Christianity and no other Gospel than the liberty both of body & mind to exercise the Divine

Arts of Imagination' William Blake

The feelings you're chasing are stained
On surfaces. Just the ink of the words.
The thin residue of the artist's pained
Personality marking the absurd
On the canvas. The scab on the skin.
The news room smile. The melodic refrain.
A doorway. An embrace. A beginning.
We each have a violent vengeance within,
Many and righteous, from which we abstain,
And dark, brooding compassion, restraining
Our vindictive entrails with humane skin.
We are a mess of history, engrained.
All this is not exhaustive of our parts,
And our whole? A yet greater work of art.

46

Pondering The Everyday Motherhood Moments by Joy A. Mead

Last night's dinner dishes were piled up in the kitchen sink, building up quickly as dirty breakfast bowls and plates were ready to join in for a morning wash. The children, still happily wearing their pajamas, were engrossed in their game of imaginative play while my husband worked out some new songs on his guitar. Still in my bathrobe myself, I briefly scanned the kitchen and family room, taking inventory of the chores to complete: the mound of growing laundry, a dishwasher to unload and reload several times, toys scattered about ready to tidy, crumbs to vacuum, homework to complete with my daughter and son, etc. I could feel my mama anxiety steadily rising as I wondered how much of a dent I might make in my to-do list before it would be lunchtime!

As I started a load of laundry, the Holy Spirit nudged me to take another look at these rooms. I paused to observe my sweet little ones blissfully full of giggles and my musically talented husband in his element being creative for a few moments. They were enjoying their Saturday morning, unphased by the scattered mess dotted about our house! So why was I allowing some normal family chaos to squash my joy? By taking a second glance, the Holy Spirit was enlarging my mental capacity and heart's lens to see beyond all the little household tasks, to clearly see the beautiful souls I get to do life with daily. In that ordinary moment, a flood of thankfulness overwhelmed me, and a joy that only came when I stopped to truly see all of the goodness around me.

Amidst the endless chores, I deliberately sat down at our kitchen table to read a devotional and the accompanying Bible verses. I followed the example of my family to momentarily stop the busy tasks and nourish my own soul. Writing in my journal, I felt like with every word written I was declaring to myself that I refused to be fully consumed by the ever-present, necessary-but-not-so-important little details of life while missing what really counts. It was a half hour of my morning well spent, and I resumed my job with a positive determination to love and serve my family to the best of my ability.

As mothers, there are many distractions with a mile-long, to-do list and so many family needs to meet—including our own. However, I pray that the Holy Spirit keeps giving me—and all of us mamas—those promptings to slow down and take in all the blessings we have before us. Just as Mary, the mother of Jesus, pondered all of the miraculous moments of Jesus' birth and the unique characters they met and were blessed by along the way, I want to be alert and attentive that each moment is a precious opportunity to embrace and appreciate time with my children.

I'm currently at the in-between season of motherhood where my children are no longer really little ones, but they haven't quite reached the pre-teen/teenager phase either. With enough years in my role of a mama, I can visually see just how quickly my babies have grown up before my eyes. My daughter and son still need me but not in the same ways as before when it was diaper changes, pushing them to the park in a stroller, and cutting up their dinner into small pieces. They are both rapidly growing in independence such as tidying up their own rooms and being able to help with basic meal preparations. Seeing their progress has made me realize that even though some days can be incredibly difficult to meet my children's physical, mental, emotional, and spiritual needs, I need to savor these days up. I want to gather and hold dear to my heart all the everyday motherhood moments.

So whatever motherhood season you find yourself in, I encourage you to treasure every moment you have with your children, who will spread their wings into the many phases of childhood and eventually soar through life as they reach adulthood before you know it! Just like the Holy Spirit prompted me to stop worrying about all of the household tasks to complete and instead focus on the important things, I pray that your eyes would be open to see your children for all of who they are now and all the potential of who they will become later.

Each squeezy cuddle, a snuggle while reading a bedtime story, an encouraging word, a board game played, a Bible story shared, a prayer to say thank you or ask for help, and each jigsaw puzzle completed together are all ways that we nurture and love on our children. May God grant to each of us the ability to balance our days between everyday chores and spending quality time with our children. Each day, no matter how challenged we may feel, is a gift and opportunity to rely on God more fully in our uniquely, important roles as mothers. Let's daily invite Jesus to guide us through the joys and challenges of everyday motherhood, being awake to the wonder and beauty of our children, and thanking God for each moment as we hold them close to our hearts for eternity.

"But Mary treasured up all these things and pondered them in her heart."—Luke 2:19

47

Slough Songs by Laura Trimble

"This miry slough is such a place
as cannot be mended."
—Bunyan

Over the slough the tree swallows eddy
in eloquent curlicues scribbled on sky.

The sloughs are where you hope for birds,
along the highways stop for them, listen

for the dual-note of returning redwing
blackbirds in spring—and always find it—

scout for the infinite variety of homely
ducks in pools that replicate the sky

as only mud could do. You can hear the full
octave of life resonate in the clamber

of long wings straining to climb away.
Drain the sloughs only at your peril.

48

A Whisper to the Worn and Weary Mother by Jennifer Wier

Dear mama, do you feel depleted?

Motherhood is a sacred calling and an immeasurable blessing, one many women yearn to experience. And yet, this blessed role can be nearly all-consuming, filled with so much surrender it borders on the edge of indignity. Much of the time, a mother will barely give these sacrifices a second thought, because her first thought is for her children. Every once in a while, though, the weight of it all can feel suffocating, and the constant self-denial that motherhood asks of a woman can leave her feeling utterly spent.

I was feeling this loss of dignity sorely one night as I got the last little one down to sleep and began getting myself ready for bed. I went through the motions of minimal self-care like a mindless afterthought. I was weary, and discouragement came upon me like a tidal wave. It was triggered by something silly, maybe postpartum hair loss or hormone-induced dental issues, but it rose to the surface and the tears began to fall. I felt suddenly stung by the toll this role of mother had taken on me, what it had required of me. At that moment, it seemed that physically, mentally, emotionally, and socially, I was a shadow of the person I used to be. I felt trampled.

Every so often, I feel God speak to me—not in an audible voice, but sometimes with specific words. It could be a forgotten verse from Scripture called to mind at just the right moment, or maybe a thought so unexpected I can be sure it didn't come from me. This time, it was both.

It should have been no surprise to me that the Spirit of God would come in and speak to a discouraged mother's heart. After all, Scripture reveals to us in countless ways a God who has a heart for the worn and weary. He honors and cares for those who give of themselves to care for others, even if the world does not because that is who He is Himself—one who loves to the point of laying down his own life. Nonetheless, I was taken by surprise when I heard Him say it as I stood looking at my own reflection in the mirror: **"Every valley will be lifted up, and every mountain will be made low."**

"Every valley shall be raised up, every mountain and hill made low; the rough ground shall become level, the rugged places a plain. And the glory of the Lord will be revealed, and all people will see it together." (Isaiah 40:4-5)

Mountains low. Valleys high. I was awestruck by these unexpected words, and the truth they revealed was this: God esteems not the lofty but the lowly. The Lord looks with great affection on those who choose to bow their hearts and bend their knees to serve in love, and He promises to lift up their heads. To those who will humble themselves in this way, God promises favor, regard, honor, exaltation, and grace *(Ps.138:6, Prov. 3:34, Prov.29:23, Mt. 23:12, Lk. 1:52, Ja.4:6, 1 Pet. 5:5).*

This realization was a healing balm for the soul, soothing me that night and in the days to come. God saw me, a lowly mother, just as He saw the dishonored young mother Hagar in the desert, and He spoke words of comfort. Mary sang it, too, as she embraced both the unimaginable blessing and the worldly disgrace the gift of motherhood would bring her: the Lord has been mindful of the humble state of his servant (Lk.1:48). If the act of loving generously through humble service is what pleases the Lord, then what a precious gift we mothers possess— a humble position that affords us the opportunity to delight Him daily as we give of ourselves to care for these vulnerable ones He has entrusted to us.

Caretakers need care, too, however, and the Lord himself will sweetly tend to our needs as we come to Him—the fount of Living Water— for refreshment. Oh, how much we need this living water! And therein lies another great blessing: only those who are stretched beyond their capacity become aware enough of their need for Him that they come and drink. Heaven knows a weary mother is stretched beyond her limits, and yet she is so very close to Jesus in her need. What a marvelous thing it is that the humbling work which causes us to thirst for refreshment would be the very thing that offers us a path to closeness with God!

This is good news for me, a lowly mother who knows deep down, despite my occasional discouragement and doubt, that my life, my role, and my children have immeasurable value in God's eyes. I know, too, that He placed me in this humbling position for good and beautiful purposes: that I might bow my heart low in worship, letting go of my pride, vanity, and selfishness (oh how tightly I cling to it sometimes...). That my eyes would be opened to the things that really matter. That I would be refined to be made more like Him and revel in the privilege of participating in His Kingdom work, not the least of which are the precious children before me. And above all, I must remember my need for Jesus, depending on Him to walk me through the hard days.

Sweet mama, there will be days when your role feels far from honorable, but the opportunity to get down on your knees to invest in these little ones whom God values so highly is, in fact, a great honor. He chose you for this high and holy calling of motherhood, and it's worth so much more than fancy clothes or college degrees. God sees you and esteems you, even when you look and feel entirely un-put-together. He has chosen the humble all along— lowly shepherds, unwed mothers, contrite sinners, little brothers, fishermen, and little children. He calls them the greatest because they look most like Jesus.

49

My Glory is Before Thee by A.M. Everett

"Stand firm My glory is before thee
Take heart for I am Lord of all
In me find joy and peace abounding
For I have ransomed your soul"

Pain hath no fight,
Nor death it's victory
When Jesus Christ,
Be in whose name I plea.
Then only life and love I find in Him,
He whose wounds bought my redemption.

He, who for me, was pierced and broken,
Now sits upon His rightful throne.
And I though just a lowly servant,

Shall one day come to Him atoned.

There in His presence lay my pain and strife.
Then shall I join the creatures of the light.
In singing praises, shouting victory.
The name of Christ, my all sufficient plea.

What Lord should I, when on Your face am gazing,
Count wasted; mourn as lost?
No thing no moment spent for glory,
But those declared, "too high a cost."

He in whose majesty I stand complete
Once sacrificed His throne and died for me.
And so shall I, though nothing in compare
Commit my all into His care.

50

The Love of Grief by
Ravanna Dee Steinke

Being exposed to the world of grief was a lot like that time I jumped off a bridge at one o'clock in the morning during my post-prom adventures. The ground had been snow-free for a week, so the initial shock felt like knives along every inch of my skin. I vividly remember the jump off the railing, how the wind caught at any exposed skin, and the regretful plunge down. It was much deeper and darker than I had imagined. Swept up in fear, I suddenly thought, *"Why in the world did I do this?"* I began kicking hard and couldn't break to the surface fast enough. The water was so cold, and my thought was purely on survival, *"keep swimming up."* By the time I reached the air, I was gasping towards the night sky. I was alive, and I just needed to reach the riverbank to ensure I stayed that way.

Losing my triplets felt a lot like that. Though instead of jumping, I was shoved forcefully over the ledge. Struggling in the depth of it. In fact, in some ways, I'm still "swimming up." Waiting to break to the surface—for the promise of Jesus and eternity with them. Knowing I'm missing a lifetime with them feels a lot like sitting at the bottom of that icy river. There's little warmth in it. It's a million "what if's" caught up in the memory of bleeding and sobbing over a toilet. It's an absence in every family photo and a longing to know all the details of their features. As much as it has become familiar to carry, the gravity of grief can hit me like a startled gasp into a frozen plunge.

In the beginning, before there was any certainty as to why I was bleeding from an invisible wound, I held onto the truth that God raises the dead and works unexpected miracles. I prayed as any desperate mother would. With a relentless passion that, once again, Jesus would move. But with the conflicting evidence hidden in every cramp and bathroom run, I grew wearier. My hope and confusion morphed into rage as the bleeding continued. *"How could You give me these wonderful babies, and then let them die?"* I felt betrayed by my body, my faith, and by God. After the loss of our son, Oliver, a few years prior, I'd been told it was a fluke. One in four couples experience a miscarriage and it was unlikely to ever happen again. Yet, again, it had. In desperation, I begged God to change my circumstance.

Then, on the most horrible Saturday, I stood in our white linoleum shower as blood streamed in rivulets down my legs. It hit me. My Mighty God, who I knew to be unchanging and, therefore, remained good and Holy even in the midst of my suffering, wasn't going to answer my prayers in the way I so dearly wanted. His perfect will looked different than my precious desire to keep my babies. It remains the most shattering moment of my life. That feeling of lost hope, mixed into pink water as I scrubbed viciously at the dried blood. Watching it swirl down a silver drain—knowing I could do nothing to change it. Powerless, alone, and now a tomb to three longed-for babies—I felt empty in every way. When I reflect back, I see this as the moment when God began a new work in me. Where I began to see gratitude in a den of despair.

For even as I grieve them, I am thankful. I am thankful for the short weeks of pure joy after months of praying for those two lines. I am thankful for the soft, cotton, "BIG Bro" shirt that I pull out when I feel their absence. I am grateful for the contractions that birthed two of my three babies into my shaking hands and for the extra weeks of spotting that stretched my heart toward ruin as my third baby came apart in pieces. For as awful as it all was, it made those sweet babies more real. The pain was a physical reminder of how much my body hated losing them, too. Every day, my grief reminds me of how incredibly grateful I am for their miraculous life. But mostly, I am thankful that God revealed how this suffering was birthing in me something completely different than my babies—a righteousness that rises from the ruin of misplaced hopes. A freedom that comes with worshiping the Promiser over the promise, however good the promise may be.

To really *know* God, I had to relearn who I am to Him. I needed to believe His characteristics were not only real but were the foundation of everything. I needed to become aware of my absolute need for Jesus. I didn't know it at the time but my faith had been weak. Weak faith that was built on fragile ideas of prayer and church attendance. God didn't take my children away, the presence of sin in our broken world did. I rest assured that Jesus conquered death. He is and always has been for life. Though God, in His great wisdom, chose not to intervene, a reunion *will* occur. I know now, even in grief, His decision is the only one that has both my walk of faith and the heavenly kingdom in perfect mind.

"He has made everything beautiful in its time. Also, He has put eternity in their hearts, except that no one can find out the work that God does from the beginning to end." (Ecclesiastes 3:11)

I wait on the Lord in this grief. For if He said it, it is true. In time, all things will be made beautiful. Even in the wrongness of this world, in the tragedy and longing, God is working. In the events of my life, from His divine perspective, there is nothing too ugly for Him to restore and use. I believe He puts eternity on our hearts, not because it brushes off the events in our life as unimportant in comparison to Eternity with Him, but because He is a God of compassion and love. Our hearts need the hope that no loss is greater than the joy He has planned to come. No pain will be forgotten by the Great Comforter. Every tear *will* be dried.

My babies died, and in the shattering loss of their lives, I have grown to know a joy that hides in the vapor of everyday life. It makes my God-gifted roles and responsibilities that much more significant in this temporary world. I see His refinement in me every time I respond gently to my husband and care for my rainbow son, and now daughter, in the Spirit of prayer. I've seen Him rise up in my heart as King and Savior when my first thought was to forgive instead of shame. Each time I respond in love, rather than act out in impatience as I'd once have, I marvel at His work. As I reflect on how my heart has grown towards Jesus, I see the gift that lives in the aftermath of my loss. With every minute, hour, and day that this brokenness draws me nearer to Jesus and to the hope of His kingdom, grief becomes a tool of deliverance. For that, I will love this grief and the sweet babies that introduced me to it.

51

Thin Space by Elizabeth Wickland

I am a thin space,
thick of skull
and of waist
though I am,
a temple:
Where the God of heaven
makes a home
in the dust of the earth,
Where the Divine
puts on flesh
and moves into the neighborhood.
I am a thin space,
bringing the temple to those
who wouldn't step inside,
offering His hands to those

who wouldn't meet His eyes,
planting the seeds of love
and joy and peace
that grow into paradise,
not a place, but a person.
I am a thin space;
and may I become thinner,
liminal, numinous,
as He shines clearer.

52

Micah by Sarah Soltis

"Woe is me! for I am as when they have gathered the summer fruits, as the grape-gleanings of the vintage: there is no cluster to eat: my soul desired the firstripe fruit." (Micah 7:1 KJV)

A grape-gatherer searches
shriveled row after shriveled
row. Stomach empty, hands
emptier, he listens:
the dirge the crow squaws stings.
First-ripe cluster fills,
for a moment, the hungry mind
with the red relief shaking fingers cannot find.
But light in this vineyard cannot lie:
good fruit has perished. There is
only hope, now, to eat.

53

Persevere by Trusting in God by Deborah Rutherford

By leaning on God, we find all we need. We move courageously and boldly from discouraged to encouraged and persevering by trusting in God.

I woke up this morning feeling discouraged. My neck hurt as I thought about yesterday's disappointing email. Was I just spinning my wheels? My hand brushed hard against the door as I retreated to the solace of my bedroom. Hidden away from the eyes of rejection.

As I propped myself up on pillows to read my Bible I felt God say, "Rest." God was with me as I dozed— soothing, and loving me. He was saying *it is going to be OK, don't worry. Your job is to show up every day and do your best.* But I confess I just wanted to quit and give up for a moment. Not necessarily forever, just for a moment, but that's not what God calls us to do.

After resting, I read Psalm 58 from "Spurgeon and the Psalms." Although I had not received any instruction or insights from the Holy Spirit, I thought I would move on. But then I felt convicted to read Psalm 58 in my "Charles F. Stanley Life Principles Bible," where there are always good study notes to gleam. When I read Psalm 58:11, there I found my instruction and direction. *"So that men will say, "Surely there is a reward for the righteous; Surely He is God who judges in the earth."*

Throughout the Bible, God promises to reward His faithful people beyond what their deeds deserve. What a beautiful promise that I needed to cling to. The study notes pointed to Revelation 22:12, *"Look, I am coming soon! My reward is with me, and I will give to each person according to what they have done."* Then, in Matthew 6:19-21, we are told we are storing treasures in heaven that no one can ever take away from us.

It does not matter how small our work is, if it may seem insignificant, or if nobody notices. Because God sees. We are a part of His beautiful plan, great recipe, and the big picture. Extraordinary relief washes over me, and then, in my mind, I see the word *perseverance*. I knew right then that God wants me and you, too, to persevere. Persevere by trusting in God. Don't give up. Don't quit. And He will give guidance, direction, and instruction. Perseverance with the One who loves you. God will bring us through our discouragement, problems, or any obstacle. This perseverance sustains us on our sanctification walk leading to eternal salvation.

When we are weak, discouraged, or disillusioned, God asks us to lean on Him. And by leaning on God, I received a nap, which is precisely what I needed.

We are homemakers, in the office, out in the field, and creatives, all struggling to balance family, work, and faith. Although we may often feel unqualified, we don't have to be qualified, just willing to follow. We can honor God and push forward with confidence and clarity. Thankfully we are not alone on this journey.

God knew I was feeling discouraged, so He lifted me. First, He gave me the direction to rest. Then the instruction to persevere. On top of that, He filled me with joy, peace, and relief. And He will do that for you too.

What will you do when life casts defeat, discouragement, or disappointment? From disappointing emails to crushing phone calls to an unwanted change. Will you give up, run away, or lean on the Father God? Will you trust Him?

But there is a better way—we can come to God for rest, guidance, and instruction. Let Him fill us with all we need as we courageously and boldly balance and persevere with love for our families, home, and faith.

God always provides exactly what we need. Sometimes it is as simple as a nap.

54

After Repentance by Jessica Mangano

"He's closer than my breath."

This hope clings to me as fresh snow to the naked oaks I pass. I'm grateful and afraid. I owe everything now - no part of me hidden, no part mine - if my form weren't this twisted I wouldn't care. But I know the aged, warped maple at the trailhead is my companion. Warped, bent back on herself and writhing, her knotted scars disturbingly evident in the late winter sun. Even then, the ink green saplings bring a sense of revelry. It's coming soon.

It must.

My tightening ribs and the shameful catch of my breath say so. It must, it must...beneath my singed pride, relief presses through in every inhale.

Winter herself catches a single, great breath, pressing into dense and tender silence as the woods recover, as the bare trees quake. Winter and her Father, Exposer of every hastily closed wound, of every fruitful and barren branch. Even when tonight's winter sky is starless as a child lacking her childhood, we're seen. We're crippled. We're adored. We're made whole.

Rejoice.

55

Mercy on Main Street by Marilyn Gardner

I can see the house in my mind—a large, yellow Victorian with green trim. It stands solid on Main Street in the small town of Essex, Massachusetts. For over 180 years the house has stood there, watching over families and life, providing shelter and a physical address, and offering its occupants a tangible place to call home.

For six of those years, the house on Main Street was our home. On the day we moved in, my husband carried 36 years and however many pounds of me over the threshold, followed by our five kids, excitedly rushing past us to claim bedrooms and explore all the spaces that an old house offers to children with vivid imaginations.

The house was magnificent. Thirty-six windows allowed light into every corner, beveled glass in doorways brought elegance from bygone days, and a claw-foot bathtub was nestled under eaves in a tiny upstairs bathroom. A big kitchen on the main floor connected to a combined living/dining room, while a past renovation had connected a barn to the right side of the house, transforming it into two upstairs bedrooms and a family room. Clear on the other side was another staircase that took you from the official front door up to a second level with more bedrooms and, hidden under the eaves, a perfect Harry Potter closet. A second kitchen to the left of the stairs and another family room allowed more space than the seven of us thought possible.

On the day we moved in, early September sunshine radiated off polished wood floors and I thought my heart would break from the beauty of all of it. We had a place to call our own and the quintessential American address: 2 Main Street.

We had never owned a home before. We spent our first 12 years of marriage traversing the globe, having babies, and living in tall apartment buildings with no elevators. We knew what it was to pack our bags and head out into the unknown, creating space and place out of nothing, but making sure that photo albums and at least one precious possession for each member of the family made it into our cargo.

Most recently, we had hung our hearts in Cairo, Egypt and our move to Massachusetts was not an easy one. We spent the year before we moved to 2 Main Street in a rental home on the other side of town. While the house was ugly and the kitchen a blinding orange, our kids found solace in a pond in the backyard. Our kids could be whoever they wanted to be on the pond. Whether sunshine, snow, or rain, they were out on the pond, sometimes as pirates and other times as explorers, but always as children in transition with a deep need for the unconditional comfort that nature brings.

The transition year was chaotic and full of grief. We missed the warmth and palm trees of our beloved Egypt, and the dog days of summer in other parts of the country became the dog days of winter for us in Massachusetts. They were interminable, passing by as slowly as an old woman walking with a cane. We also tried to deal with marriage wounds that had long been hidden but slowly resurfaced, even as we tried to squash them down.

We had lived in the rental house for ten months when we found out two things: our landlord was selling it and there was a large Victorian home for sale up the road. The idea of owning a home filled us with dread for how grownup it sounded, and delight for the thought of a permanent address. Miraculously, for we had neither the income nor the money to afford it, the bank and the owner accepted our meager offer, and we began packing our bags for our supposed "forever home."

When we moved to 2 Main Street, we felt we had left all the transition and chaos of the international move behind. This was a second chance, a new beginning. We were moving to a space that would become our own. My husband looked at me and said, "They can carry me from this house to the graveyard out back. I am not moving again." Raised in a military family, this was his 30th house in 36 years. He, along with our entire family, was ready for stability, peace, and a place to put our books. Here we would heal and grow and become whole.

* * *

Essex, Massachusetts is a small town of three thousand people. The quaint, coastal town proudly claims the title of America's antique capital. With over 35 stores within a mile of each other, the name is well-earned. Enter any one of the stores and you will find old bureaus, 18th-century desks, and chipped Royal Albert China cups all covered in a thin layer of dust. Browse further and there will be more treasures—old clocks and paintings of undetermined worth are perched on grandma's attic furniture, and there is always a basket of crocheted doilies.

Along with old antiques, Essex has its abundance of old restaurants and equally as many old attitudes, attitudes that did not take kindly to a family of outsiders moving into their precious space. There were the "townies" and the outsiders. We quickly learned who we were.

"The other day a Moroccan woman served me!" said a townie to my husband one day as they met at the local Dunkin' Donuts, followed by an emphatic "Who lets these people in?" "Well, who let you in?" said my husband. "My people came on the Mayflower," he proudly declared! And that one conversation described Essex perfectly.

Most of the time we were happily oblivious, blindly thinking we were well loved. We threw ourselves into the town activities: Soccer on Saturday mornings in the fall, baseball on Saturday mornings in the spring, and every October, a clam chowder festival featuring restaurants from all the surrounding towns, competing for the coveted prize of best clam chowder. We lived an outside life that shouted perhaps too loudly "Hey! Look at us! We belong" even as our life inside was full of food, surroundings, and worldviews that originated miles from 2 Main Street.

During the weekdays, our lives revolved around school activities, and during most weekends, you would find our family sitting in the front pews of the First Congregational Church of Essex, established in 1663. During renovations in 1852, the church hung a bell made by Paul Revere, and to this day it rings out on Sunday mornings, reminding all who heard it that despite popular Pew polls proclaiming the dearth of Christians in Massachusetts, some people still attended church. At times, my mind would wander away from the church service and a semi-melodic choir with a high-pitched soprano, and I would wonder—if this was the first congregational church, where was the second, but I never found out. One was sufficient for me.

* * *

We had moved to 2 Main Street with fractured hearts and a wounded marriage. While the surface wounds scabbed over, the deeper ones grew deeper still. The busyness of two working adults doing the important work of raising five children did not leave time for the even more crucial work of healing a marriage. And then there was Essex itself. The harder I tried, the less I belonged. We opened our home every other Friday night for couples to come and eat dessert and talk, "Dessert and Dialogue" we called it, and the pithy name worked. 2 Main Street was a popular Friday night destination in a town that rolled up its proverbial carpets and shut its doors by five in the evening. We directed plays at the school; my husband told stories about ancient Egypt in living color to middle schoolers; I led small groups at the church. But I was always getting it wrong, not reading social cues, and offending the good ancestors of the Mayflower.

Pull up your bootstraps—said a friend of mine. Quit whining; adjust, when in Rome… the clichés hurt my soul, stunting my ability to connect. I tried and then tried again. But fractured hearts and wounded souls are bootless, so no matter how hard you try, you cannot pull up your bootstraps and live well.

And then the severe mercy of God swept over us in a mighty wave. It was Christmas time and we had picked out the perfect Christmas tree. Others were either too tall or too top-heavy, resembling oddly drawn cartoon characters, but the one we picked had none of those characteristics. It was perfect. It stood in the bay windows of our house at 2 Main Street, its bright lights masking the pain in our home. The hidden wounds of our marriage became an open crisis, and we could no longer pretend. Loss of jobs and any reputation we thought we had threw us into God's arms. We needed a hospital for our souls, and the church down the street was not that hospital.

* * *

No one talks about the taste of pain. It is bitter and bile-like, affecting everything you eat so that nausea floods over you and nothing tastes good. Not even the pink and green frosted sugar cookies that I had in abundance; my grandmother's recipe, made with confectioner's sugar instead of regular. Constant nausea met with a constricting throat, and I would cry, my tears from such a deep place that they came out in anguished sobs. There was no more mercy to draw from; there was no more grace to give. We were like burn victims; our emotional skin was covered in blistering wounds. No matter what anyone did to help us, we would scream in pain and anger, verbally screaming at them to go away, silently begging them to stay.

And all the while, the people of Essex went about their good and righteous ways. "There were a lot of lights left on in your house over the weekend! Don't you know what electricity costs these days?" "I saw your daughter's legs through the upstairs window. You may want to tell her to pull her shades down." "Will you be helping with the spaghetti dinner next year? We sure could use your help! It takes everyone you know." "Will you be shoveling your sidewalk? You know every house needs to take responsibility for the sidewalk in front of them."

Can you not hear my silent screams? Can you not give us grace? But my loud cries remained silent and the wider world of Essex beyond 2 Main Street did not feel safe.

* * *

Deep physical wounds go through four dynamic stages or phases of wound healing. The four phases are hemostasis, the inflammatory phase, the proliferation phase, and the maturation phase.

Hemostasis is the first response of the body to injury. The body is, in a sense, on high alert and forms blood clots to stop the bleeding and control the injury. Quickly afterward comes the inflammatory stage. This is when the wound is red and warm, it hurts, and we want to cry as well as guard it. Beyond the pain, the body is working hard to repair by getting antibodies, nutrients, and white blood cells to the wounded area. This is a painful stage, and we react accordingly.

The proliferation stage is the beginning of rebuilding. The wound begins to granulate from the bottom up, closing in and healing along the way. Essential to this process is that the wound has proper nutrients and oxygen supplied by blood vessels. If you cut off the oxygen supply, then you jeopardize the healing process.

Maturation is the last phase. This continues the process of rebuilding but takes it a step further to complete healing—this process works to remodel and refashion the wound. It is important to remember that this process of complete healing can take up to two years. This is a critical time. Wounds may look like they have healed but if one is not careful, they can break down.

The process of emotional wound healing is similar. How well I remember that hemostasis phase of our wounds, where we fought to control the damage, only to realize how deep it went and how long it would take to create hemostasis. We went through days in a blur, unable to eat or sleep. We numbly took down the name of a counselor, driving an hour and a half in a blizzard only to get lost and end up in his office five minutes before the end of the first session. We equally numbly made our next appointment for the next day, and then drove to a Burger King, ravenous yet unable to eat but a few bites.

We moved on to the inflammatory stage, our hearts so raw we could not hide the wound. The inflammation and pain were too great. We jerked back when people tried to get close because we were so afraid they would further wound us. In all of this, the lights and radio music of Christmas and New Year's mocked us with their good cheer and flippant hope.

In the middle of that life-altering wound, close friends and family brought oxygen and nutrients for the proliferation phase. They drew close, ignoring our pushing away. They steadily walked beside us and brought life to our hurting souls. They were our wound healers, gatherers of pain, and givers of comfort. The broader world of Essex may have seemed cruel, but inside 2 Main Street, light still filtered through the tall windows that had brought light in for so many years. A wood-burning stove still gave off heat and the glow of live coals in the dead of night. Wooden floors still radiated light from the sun.

Sometimes we thought we would never truly heal, but time went on, and the proliferation stage silently, significantly did its work. We reached Phase Four unexpectedly and unassumingly – this was the stage of Remodeling. Like Narnia under the spell of the White Witch, where winter lasted forever, and spring was a distant dream for old Narnians, so was the idea of healing. And then, like the Beaver's whisper that Aslan was on the move, suddenly the whispered hope of remodeling was upon us.

Just as the last stage in wound healing is not obvious to the casual observer, this remodeling of our hearts and souls did not show; it was the people close to us who knew it was taking place. The casual observer of 2 Main Street still commented on our use of electricity; still gossiped in the local library about "that family at 2 Main Street." The blood and inflammation were gone, but the remodeling was actively taking place, our hearts began to beat with new life, becoming warm. The scars were there, but they became well-storied scars that spoke of hurt and pain but radiated healing. Best of all, our ears were now deaf to gossip.

* * *

My husband never made it from the house to the graveyard. We moved on from Essex after six years, to another state, another house, another life. When we moved back to Massachusetts after a few years away, we found ourselves driving through Essex on the way to a nearby town on a summer day. The sky was the same deep blue that it had been the day we moved into 2 Main Street. My husband drove slowly past the house, and we all fell silent, each of us reliving our own memories. The new owners had chopped down two Maple trees in the yard along with the hedges that blocked us off from the busy streets. The house looked dilapidated and sad, void of life with no kids playing in the yard. The porch was empty of wicker furniture and dollhouses. Despite all the pain, the house still radiated life during our time there—all of life, the good and the tragic, the beautiful and the painful.

I felt the old but familiar taste of pain on my tongue as we drove past. As incarnate beings, we are bound to place, and it is integrally connected to whatever is happening in our lives at the time. A quaint, coastal town, boasting antique shops and a plethora of restaurants would never be the way I saw Essex. Instead, it was a place that shouted of pain and only whispered redemption, a place that shouted of hurt and lack of belonging and only whispered healing.

In Alicia Paddock's work on sacred space, she talks about space being an abstract concept, that it needs an identity and memories to change it to 'place'. The identity and memories attached to Essex were painful, and while space had indeed become place in that beautiful house, the cost was high and the memories were not always sweet.

In the book *One Live Coal to the Sea*, author Madeleine L' Engle explores mercy and grace in the life of a family. In beautiful prose, she describes mercy in the midst of evil and dysfunction, mercy despite selfishness and betrayal, and mercy when life demands judgment. The book's title comes from a quote by William Langland *"But all the wickedness in the world which man may do or think is no more to the mercy of God than a live coal dropped in the sea."* We were one live coal to the mercy of God, mercy that defied the smallness of the town's borders, stretching far beyond to the nearby ocean.

Through my years of healing, I have come to see Essex as a place that represents God's great and severe mercy, for that mercy enveloped us at 2 Main Street. It no longer matters that it is a place that held so many wounds, a place that scarred our hearts, for the price of scars is small compared to the generosity of mercy and the grace of healing.

* * *

Sometimes it comes up in conversation that we used to live in Essex. "Essex!" people exclaim. "That's a beautiful little town!" I pause before I answer. In my mind, I travel up Main Street and turn into the driveway. The side porch sits with its dollhouse painted just like the house and its white wicker furniture. I enter the side doorway and take a moment to look in on my memories, both good and hard, and the stories that this magnificent old house holds from our family. The hidden wounds and joys, the world of a couple in pain, trying to hold it together until they no longer could. I quickly travel through the long years of mercy and healing, the grace of God so definitive and true, finally arriving at my answer. "Yes, it is a beautiful little town."

56

Divine Kisses of Grace by Dawn Kopa

Kevin and I awoke before dawn in order to ride to the top of the nearby peak in time to catch the sunrise. He made a quick breakfast and as we sat at the table, he strongly encouraged me to eat, even though I didn't have an appetite that early in the morning. He insisted that my body would need the fuel because we had a full, active day planned. I obliged, and I'm glad I did, because I didn't know yet the events that were about to transpire, nor that it would be at least a full 24 hours before I'd even think about food again.

After breakfast, we took off on a couple of ATVs, following a trail that led from the back of his cabin up into the nearby Aspen grove. I was visiting him in Taos, New Mexico for an extended Memorial Day weekend adventure trip. While I'd spent a fair amount of time in the Appalachian Mountains and backpacking in the Rockies, I'd never seen anything yet like the unmatched glory of an Aspen grove in the summer—much less the majesty of *getting to watch the sunrise* from the top of a mountain standing in the middle of one.

When we returned to the cabin from chasing the sun, for some reason which was out of character for me, I wanted to call my mom. I was a 26-year-old free-spirited rambler who went where the wind blew. I liked to be fully present where I was and didn't usually use the phone much while traveling. But on this day, something was different.

Kevin let me use the cabin phone; there wasn't any cell service in the mountains where we were staying anyways. The phone only rang one time before my mom answered in a frenzy. "Dawn," she said, "I've been trying to reach you all night. It's about your dad...Dawn, your dad is dead." I felt the wind get knocked out of my gut and the strength leave my legs, buckling to the floor. When I asked what happened, she told me, "He shot himself." Before I could even process that, the next words were flying out of my mouth, *"What about Bobby?"*

Bobby is my half-brother, my father's son from another marriage after his divorce from my mom. He had just turned 12 years old at this time, and he and my father lived alone together in another state. I'd only met Bobby in person 3 times before. I would soon come to learn that he was in the house when my father took his life, and even worse, that he was the one who found our dad dead in the front seat of his car parked in the dark garage with a gunshot wound to his chest. Our dad had told him he was going to the grocery store, and after too much time had passed, Bobby started to get worried and went looking for him. He hadn't heard the sound of the gunshot because he had been in the back of the house playing Grand Theft Auto on his PlayStation with the volume on the TV turned pretty high. Bobby didn't know what to make of what he saw, and ran to his friend's house down the street. The parents called 911, and eventually the authorities in Oklahoma, where they lived, were able to track down an address in Houston, where I lived.

My dad and Bobby lived in a city where there was no family–my dad had retired from the USAF there, and then just never left. So, while Bobby was with a foster family, he really didn't have anyone to permanently take him in there. The police officer who'd contacted my mom in Houston was looking for any next-of-kin who could come and claim him. I knew I had to get to Oklahoma immediately.

It was a four-hour drive from the cabin to the nearest airport. I hastily threw my stuff in my bag and Kevin started driving me right away. I only remember two things about that drive. That I couldn't do any of the things that needed to be done, like book a flight to Oklahoma, because there was no cell service for most of the drive. And that I'd have gone crazy if not for a divine kiss of grace just a few months prior to this.

Six months prior, my good friend Kevin was moving away from Houston. After I bid him farewell standing in the parking lot of Terry Hershey Park next to his blue Subaru, as I got in my car to leave, I looked down at a CD that I thought I should give him for his road trip to New Mexico. It was *Beautiful Jesus* by Jeremy Riddle, and it was my favorite CD at the time. Even though it was 2014, I still hadn't made the transition to streaming music yet, and the only music I listened to was still on CDs. Even though I knew I would miss this particular CD, I'd hoped that the worship would be a blessing to my friend on his journey. Turns out, he didn't care for the music and never made it past the first song—his music taste was the opposite of mine with no overlap whatsoever. But he also never took the CD out of his car, and now, *it was in his car. With me.* On the four-hour drive toward something completely un-known and unexpected in the midst of what felt at the time like a shattered world.

I call this one of many divine kisses of grace that got me through that storm. It was a minor yet significant bit of refuge from the torrents of my own thoughts that otherwise would have run wild and taken me down a dark path.

As I felt waves of guilt attempt to wash over me with the thought *If only I had called him this week, maybe this wouldn't have happened...*the beautiful songs of worship coming through the Subaru speakers caught me and helped me to fix my gaze upon Jesus instead. *There's a light inside of me, it makes the darkness bright. It gives me hope when I am lost and leads me through the night.* A few moments of relief came from the guilt that is only known by many a loved one of those who have chosen to leave this world too soon.

A short while later, my thoughts tried to stray again to a place that made me feel like I wanted to crawl under a rock forever. *What if I had loved my dad better, visited more often, and made more of an effort?* I'd hear, *Jesus you alone are the Light. Jesus, bring me home again.*

Then just as this thought would make me feel like I want to vomit, *I forgot to send Bobby a birthday gift in the mail last month, maybe that really upset him,* but the lyrics would catch my attention and refocus my gaze. *The closer I come, the more of You I see, the more I cry, take all of me. All I have, I count as lost, as I fall in tears at the foot of the cross. For who am I that I could ever deserve this love. The closer I come, the more of You I see, the more that I long for you to reign in me...and all my life I gladly give to You.*

These words were more than worship. They were the very prayers lying within me that I'd otherwise not have had the words to express. *You gave me life, now take my life and live yours through me. I surrender. Lord, I surrender.*

*What's going to happen with Bobby? Will he be okay? How on earth will he ever be able to process such trauma...*As that fear opened the door for the queasiness to quickly well up, I'd hear, *Here is my heart,*

I give it to you. Please take it and break it and make it anew. I've nothing to offer that you have not given.

A continual back and forth of my mind straying and my heart pulling it back, an effortful fixating on the Lord, an intentional surrender to Him having His way with my life so that by the end of the drive, there wasn't any room for fear about what the coming days, weeks, or years would look like with me now being responsible for a kid who wasn't my own.

Once I got through security at the airport, I couldn't make it to a bathroom stall fast enough before I was on the floor weeping in a puddle of tears. A stranger stood outside the stall door and asked if I was okay and then handed me a paper towel under the door. The short Hispanic woman who helped me book a seat on the next flight out ignored the long line building up behind me and walked out from behind the ticket counter, wrapped her arms around me as a mama would, and whispered in my ear, "I will hold you in my heart and in my prayers". More divine kisses of grace.

Bobby had been staying at his friend's house down the street for the 24 hours it took for me to get to Oklahoma. The friend's parents happened to be registered with the state as foster parents, so the local CPS decided to leave him with the family until his own family could come and get him.

Bobby's mom was still alive, but had been out of his life and not seen him for several years. Between my older brother and I, we somehow knew I'd be the one to care for Bobby. It wasn't ever even a discussion. There wasn't even a time when we sat down to consider what any of this meant. What the future would look like. The level of sacrifice involved. No one around me told me to pause and think. What other option was there anyways? If I hadn't taken him, what would have happened to him? Where would he have ended up? In foster care?

When I showed up at his friend's house, he was hiding. Although he was 11, he was so small and young for his age—still very much a boy and quite a way from puberty. He popped his blonde head out from a room in the back where he had been hiding and peered at me with his big blue eyes. His head was still large for his body. He scurried out from behind the door frame and hid behind another wall...then peeked out again.

It was just a few days of the fuzzy haze that comes when handling a family tragedy. Too many logistics to consider and decisions to make to process or even grieve yet. Emptying my father's whole entire house of stuff, planning a funeral, plus being interviewed by CPS and having background checks done before they would release Bobby into my care...oh, and then also now having to take care of a kid. Thankfully, I wasn't alone. My older brother and my mom had driven up from Houston and met me in Oklahoma, and we somehow navigated through the murky waters of those days together.

Literally overnight, I went from being a free-spirited 26-year-old to having full custody of a young boy. I had no idea what all the coming years would look like, and maybe my living moment-by-moment-without-much-foresight nature of mine served me well in this regard. It enabled me to accept this present moment without much worry or concern about the future (about my own, anyways, even though I would soon come to know immense amounts of concern for his future and well-being lol). Even though I didn't know in my mind what was to come, I see now that God had been preparing me, and just how present and near He was to us at every step of the way.

Just a few days ago it was Christmas morning. It's been about nine years since that boy came into my life as my inheritance. He helped me go from being a somewhat flighty free spirit to a committed and grounded woman with roots, quite literally overnight. I had bacon frying on the stove, cinnamon rolls resting on the counter, and cookies baking in the oven. Bobby was home from college for winter break. He sat in the living room on the couch quoting lines from his old favorite movie, cracking jokes, and making me laugh, like always. His stuff was spread out all over the living room. I didn't mind, because it was just a sign that he was here, and that he feels at home. Once the cinnamon rolls were frosted and cooled, he came into the kitchen for a plate of Christmas breakfast. When I handed it to him, I told him it was my privilege for the rest of his life to help feed and nourish him every time he comes home. "Eat up. You'll need the fuel; we've got a full day ahead."

57

Family Tree by Veronica Maria Jarski

I.
The oak tree stood strong,
branches uplifted like one-thousand arms,
hands holding homes and stretching towards the sun.
    We flew without fear
and rested in its embrace.
    Psalms throbbed from our throats,
burst unbridled from our hearts.
    Our tree sang in one chorus.

II.
    Then a bird forgot to fly
and became enamored by earthly worms,
turned to the tree, and tore at its tendons.
    Branches bent in grief,

the leaves died from their sadness.

Some birds took to earth
and no longer sought the sun.
Axe men predicted faith's death.

III.
The tree still stands strong,
scarred branches lifted like two-thousand arms,
hands holding homes and stretching towards the sun.
Old nests are strengthened,
new ones have been created.
Our tree is choir-filled,
soulful birdsongs overlap.
May we someday sing as one.

58

❦

Bent, but Unbroken by Annie Nardone

I live in Florida, near the Atlantic Ocean. The craggy live oak trees, which inspired this poem, are found keeping company with the palms and palmetto shrubs in parks and along roadsides. These hardy oaks are draped with Spanish moss, giving them a look of wisdom, patience, and in the case of the oaks by the seashore, strength, and fortitude. Exposed to hurricanes and sea breezes, those oaks closest to the ocean grow differently. Their trunks are thick and gnarly, leaning with the weather, while their smaller branches reach up to the sun. Even if the trunk splits in a severe storm, the oak persists by continuing to grow out of the fractures. Their perseverance inspires me as a Divine reminder of how to approach life's storms.

The live oak stretches her limbs to the sun.
Every branch, every twig,
An ever-green crown
full open in the stance
that has taken years
of struggle to achieve.
Against unrelenting winds
and torrents, always
growing, adapting.
Bent, but unbroken.

Bathed in the Light
that renews.
Refreshed, enrobed in budding leaves and coarse bark,
Buffeted, beautiful, reaching with determination.
In this tree, we see struggle and life,
in the tawny brown and emerald green visage,
Extending her branches with bravery
and endurance.

She stretches her limbs to the Son.
Every finger reaching for renewal,
Drenched in the love from above.
Pouring down
on her weary, worn-thin mind.
Warmth feeding the soul,
face tilted up,
now reflecting the light.
Renewing,
reaching earnestly
in an attitude that has taken years
to cultivate.

An attitude of praise.
Abandoning what is below,
desiring what is above.
Where true growth begins
and is nourished.
Her roots deep
in holy ground.

59

Eighteen by Madeline
Wilkins

Each evening reminds me of
Pinched places
Of not enough
Like too-small shoes
Or a cramping hunger.
We get so little time; I
want to squeeze it
From the clock.
Let each minute drip
Second by second into
My mouth
Until I hold forever
Safe in my belly.

You're the God of sufficiency
Who can make plenty of little.
Wringing water from stone,
Bread out of air, or a
Feast from two fish.

Take these crawling,
Fleeting years and turn them
Into more than enough—
Into abundance.

60

Visitation by Rebecca D. Martin

I like the way your greens and blues and
yellow and rust sing first and then the whole
structure leans in like it's listening

for the thing at which I'd imagined
you were raising your hand in wonder
or surprise before I saw you stirring

a pot and thought *food is astonishing
too, good for you,* but it turns out the water
is dense with soap and dirt. You're hot, I imagine, not

about to be transfigured by some luminant
visitation. But maybe I'm wrong and
this is where it happens. The child

of the house trusts to the ordinariness
of the day. The birds of the air know
their care will come just
when they need it.

Biographies

"The world does not need more Christian literature. What it needs is more Christians writing good literature." C.S. Lewis

Debra Fiscus is a senior Secondary Education and English Literature Major at PennWest Edinboro University in Edinboro, Pennsylvania. She is passionate about creative writing, particularly poetry and creative nonfiction. Her works often focus on God in nature and wrestling with knowing God's goodness in the midst of pain. Outside of school and work, she is a passionate equestrian, owning horses of her own and training kids how to ride on the weekends.

Alexandria Marrow is a former high school theology teacher, who now lives on a small TX homestead with her husband and four children. It is her firm belief that poetry can be found in quite ordinary things and to unearth it is a way of meeting the Creator in gratitude. Among her many loves are travel, water, books, and blues music. She is currently working on a compilation of poems and short stories, and can be found at www.alexandriamarrow.com.

Lara d'Entremont is a wife and mom to three from Nova Scotia, Canada. Lara is a writer and learner at heart—always trying to find time to scribble down some words or read a book. Her desire in writing is to help women develop solid theology they can put into practice—in the mundane, the rugged terrain, and joyful moments. You can find more of her writing at laradentremont.com.

R. L. Busséll is a poet who never thought he would bear any resemblance to a writer. He earned a Bachelor of Arts in History from the University of North Texas, works as a draftsman, and has been known to paint portraits, dabble in design, dip pen into digital ink, and ponder about the wonder of clouds. He lives in Texas with the wife of his youth and his rose.

Emma Michael is a wife, mother, and homeopathy student residing in Utah. Reading and writing poetry has been one of her lifelong joys, and she is grateful to Calla Press for the opportunity to share some of her words with you, to the glory of God.

Stephanie Gail Eagleson holds a B.A. in English, Music, and Classical Studies from Hanover College and has taught writing, poetry, grammar, and Latin for a number of years. She now homeschools her three young children, works part-time as a freelance editor, and serves her community as a certified Domestic Abuse Prevention & Recovery Advocate. Stephanie has been published in *Beyond Words Literary Magazine* and *Persephone's Daughters*, where her short story was nominated for Best of the Net, and she has a piece forthcoming at *The Vashti Initiative*. She blogs about retaining faith through trauma in a highly irregular manner at stephaniegaileagleson.com.

Dani Nichols is a writer, cowgirl, and mom of three from Central Oregon; she writes about motherhood, family, horses, and above all, the relentless nature of redemption. Her debut book for children, Buzz the Not-So-Brave, about her lovable and quirky quarter horse, was released summer of 2022. Her work has won several writing contests and has been published in Fathom Magazine, Oregon

Humanities, Reckon Review, and others. To read more from Dani, check out her newsletter at www.wranglerdani.com and @wranglerdani and @buzzthenotsobrave on Instagram.

Lee Kiblinger is a wife, mother, literature and composition teacher, and late blooming poet. She lives in a small town in Texas and spends her time reading classics, grading essays, laughing with three teenagers, and enjoying long walks. Her poetry has appeared online at *Calla Press, Agape Review*, and *Ekstasis*. You can read more of her poetry at her new blog, www.ripplesoflaughter.com.

Sandy Brannan is a wife, mother, and grandmother. She is also a writer who loves to use words to share the hope and encouragement that can only be found through faith in Jesus.

Matthew J. Andrews is a private investigator and writer. He is the author of the chapbook *I Close My Eyes and I Almost Remember*, and his poetry has appeared in *Rust + Moth, Pithead Chapel*, and *EcoTheo Review*, among others. He can be contacted at matthewjandrews.com.

Marianna Pizzini Mankle is a Montana native who now calls Nebraska home. She has an MA in Communication from Arizona State University. Her writing can be found in Kiosk, Writeresque Literary Magazine, Spoonie Journal, New Note Poetry, and more. She can be found watching reality TV with her husband when she isn't writing.

Linda McCullough Moore is the author of two story collections, a novel, an essay collection, and more than 350 shorter published works. She is the winner of the Pushcart Prize, as well as a winner and finalist for numerous national awards. Her first story collection was endorsed by Alice Munro, and equally as joyous, she frequently hears from readers who write to say her work makes a difference in their lives. For many years she has mentored award-winning writers of fiction, poetry, and memoir. She is currently completing a novel, *Time Out of Mind,* and a collection of her poetry. www.lindamcculloughmoore.com.

Caity Neuberger is a young mama hiding away in the small world of Ohio, busy crafting stories and homeschooling her recklessly imaginative children. She recently published her first book, *Let the Earth Spin,* an everyday but introspective journey into the heart of a mother and the mind of Christ—and what happens when they come together.

Stephanie Nygaard is a writer/poet living in Illinois with her husband and three daughters. She spends her days homeschooling, reading, and writing, and hopes her life and words point people to God. Besides *Calla Press,* her writing can be found at *Wallflower Journal,* *The Way Back to Ourselves,* and on Instagram @handwritten_by_stephanie.

Chelsea Barnwell is a writer, deep thinker, and avid reader. She finds joy in serving her community alongside gospel-minded followers of Jesus. She currently lives in a historic carriage house in the Blue Ridge Mountains. You can read more of her work on her blog welcometothecarriagehouse.com.

Meg Freer grew up in Montana and lives in Ontario, where she writes and teaches piano. Her work has appeared in many journals, and she is the co-author of a poetry chapbook honoring the Sisters of Providence of St. Vincent de Paul, *Serve the Sorrowing World with Joy* (Woodpecker Lane Press, 2020). Her poems have won awards in the U.S. and Canada, and she holds a Graduate Certificate with Distinction in Creative Writing from Toronto's Humber School of Writers.

Kellie Brown is a violinist, conductor, music educator, and award-winning writer whose book, *The Sound of Hope: Music as Solace, Resistance and Salvation during the Holocaust and World War II* (McFarland Publishing, 2020), received one of the *Choice* Outstanding Academic Titles award. Her words have appeared in *Earth & Altar, Psaltery & Lyre, The Primer, Agape Review, Musing*, and others. In addition to over 30 years of music ministry experience, she is a certified lay minister in the United Methodist Church and currently serves at First Broad Street United Methodist Church in Kingsport, TN. More information about her and her writing can be found at kelliedbrown.com.

Caroline Liberatore is a poet and librarian from Northeast Ohio. In these vocational spheres, she finds herself prompted to engage with interminglings of divine brilliance and day-to-day grittiness. Much of her poetry resides here, taut between transcendent utterances of the gospel and embodied conundrums. Her work has appeared in a variety of publications, including *Ekstasis, Solum Journal*, and *Amethyst Review*.

Joy Schelzel Manning resides in Lancaster, Pennsylvania with her husband and their Portuguese Water Dog. She enjoys exploring local history and art, nurturing her sourdough starter, and crafting stories. Poetry is her life-long love.

Ryan Keating is a writer, teacher, and pastor on the Mediterranean island of Cyprus. His work can be found in publications such as Saint Katherine Review, Ekstasis Magazine, Amethyst Review,

Macrina Magazine, Fathom, Vocivia, Roi Fainéant, Dreich, and Miras Dergi, where he is a regular contributor in English and Turkish.

Pam Luschei has been a Licensed Marriage & Family Therapist (LMFT) since 2000. In November of 2019, she was a co-presenter at the American Association of Christian Counselors on "Grieving a Major Family Loss" Pam has been published on the following websites;, Nothing Is Wasted (May 2020), Widow's Might (September 2020), Salt & Clay (Oct. 2020). In September 2021, her story was published in the book, Sweet Tea for the Soul: Comforting, Real-life Stories for Grieving Hearts, by DaySpring.

Nicole Byrum is a licensed marriage and family therapist with 16 years of experience as a counselor. She is the author of Remade: Living Free, Haughty to Humble, the Workbook, and Welcome Home. Nicole also maintains a blog at nicolebyrum.com as well as a podcast, 5 Minute Word. Additionally, she is the co-host of The Biblical Woman Podcast with Catherine Cooley. Nicole lives in Northwest Ohio with her husband and two children. When she's not writing, you can find her reading, running, or cooking.

Nadine Ellsworth-Moran lives in Georgia where she serves full-time in ministry. She has a passion for writing and is fascinated by the stories of the modern South unfolding all around her as she seeks to bring everyone into conversation at a common table. Her essays and poems have appeared in *Rust+Moth, Interpretation, Ekstasis, Thimble, Emrys, Structo, Kakalak,* and *Sonic Boom,* among others. She lives with her husband and four unrepentant cats.

Diane Parrish is a writer, art gallery curator, and gardener who lives in Connecticut with her husband and their Corgi, Finn. Her work has appeared in The National Gardener magazine as well as local journals and newsletters. Her debut novel, *Something Better*, will be published by TouchPointPress in October of 2023.

Mary Anne Abdo is an emergent writer of poetry. With a background in freelance journalism, she uses her poetry and photography as a source of creative expression. That reflects the many facets of what it means to be human living in these modern times. Mary Anne has a passion for art, culture, and literature. She looks forward to the next stage where these written thoughts will take her. You can follow Mary Anne on http://bluestainedglass.wordpress.com Facebook and Instagram@MaryAnne.Abdo.

Kimberly Phinney is a national award-winning AP English instructor and has been published with *Ekstasis, Fathom, Ruminate, The Dewdrop, Wild Roof, Amethyst Review,* and *Calla Press,* among others. She has her M.Ed. in English, studied at Goddard's MFA program in Creative Writing, and is currently earning her doctorate in counseling after surviving a critical illness in 2021. Visit her literary community at www.TheWayBack2Ourselves.com and on Instagram @thewayback2ourselves.

Chrissy Callahan is the writer behind Status Quo Questions blog. She holds a master's degree in Ministerial Leadership and hopes to someday help strengthen churches and believers around the world. More of her writing can be found at www.statusquoquestions.com.

Brittney Dederman is an aspiring writer who loves to journal, work out, travel, and try new things. She has always had a love for poetry and has recently started to write her own collection of poems. She earned her Bachelor of Science in business in May of 2022. She currently is earning her MBA and is working for a university.

She hopes to one day get her collection of poems published and teach business classes at a local community college.

Kirk Jordan is the Chief Photographer for the state of Arkansas; he uses pen and lens to describe the glories of the Natural State. He delights in church history, creative music, and his bride of thirty-three years. Together, Kirk and Kerry take care of her elderly parents, saddled with dementia—a subject for his forthcoming book: "Things Charlie Says."

Jordan Sleed is an author and musician. Poetry and prose have helped him pray, and he is honored to share that gift with others who seek to experience life with God. He lives in Texas with his lovely wife, Jen, and their dog, Beni.

Caitlin N. Pate is a homemaker and writer from Mississippi. She graduated from Mississippi State University with a Bachelor of Arts degree in English and has worked in childcare and education in a variety of ways. Find more of her writing on her blog: caiteamong-wildflowers.wordpress.com.

Hannah Nelson is a wife and mother living in sweet-home Alabama with her husband, Patrick, and three young children. A former English and Rhetoric teacher, Hannah has spent the past decade helping students to recognize the True, the Beautiful, and the Good in literature as well as to write and speak persuasively from a biblical worldview. As a current stay-at-home mom, Hannah enjoys the sacred role of shepherding her children's hearts and nurturing their sense of wonder and creativity. She enjoys writing poetry, prose, and prayers inspired by her faith, family, and everyday life.

Leslie Anne Bustard lives in a century-old row home in Lancaster City, PA with her husband, Ned. Here, they love to offer food and friendship to folks and collect a plethora of artwork, music, and books. They are the parents of three grown daughters. After years of homeschooling, classroom teaching, and producing high school and children's theater, she now fills her days writing and caring for loved ones. Recently *Wild Things and Castles in the Sky: A Guide to Choosing the Best Books for Children*, co-edited with daughter, Carey, and friend, Théa Rosenburg, was published. You can find her at Square Halo Books, Cultivating, The Black Barn Online, and Story Warren, as well as her website PoeticUnderpinnings.com. She is the author of *The Goodness of the Lord in the Land of the Living*.

Caitlin Deems is a self-published author and doctor of physical therapy. During the day you can find her homeschooling her children, homesteading with her husband, and working with babies and their mothers. In the evenings you can find her reading old books. She is inspired by the love of Jesus and all things timeless.

Hannah Grace M. Staton finds her identity first and foremost in being a beloved daughter of the King. Beyond that, she is a teenage writer, book reader, and music lover. Hannah Grace is passionate about church unity and writes about matters of living out one's faith.

Charissa Sylvia is a pastor's wife and homeschooling mama writing from Harrisburg, Pennsylvania. She writes on the ancient, mountain peaks surrounded by contemplative silence and profound mystery. Ok, just kidding. She writes in a small apartment looking at a busy road with rooms full of cats and kids and mysteriously spilled drinks as well as a hopeful eye towards the light and the firm belief that the ground right under her feet is holy. You can find more of her writing on Instagram at 'CharissaSylviaWriter'.

Alexis Ragan is a creative writer who delights in serving as a literary vessel for Christ's light to dwell. Passionate about poetry, music, and global missions, she joyfully intends to blend her love for writing and teaching for the sake of the Great Commission.

Linda McCullough Moore is the author of four books and more than 500 shorter bits and pieces, winner of the Pushcart prize, now assembling a poetry collection.

Sarah L. Frantz is an author, wife of 30 plus years, mother of five, and Marmee to eight grandchildren. She and her husband live on Haven Farm outside Tulsa, Oklahoma. She delights in serving others at Jesus' table through penned words, actions of love and encouraging conversation.

J.D. Isip published his first collection of poetry, *Pocketing Feathers*, with Sadie Girl Press (2015). His second collection, *Kissing the Wound*, is forthcoming from Moon Tide Press (2023). The poems included here are part of a new project tentatively titled *All Your Billows and Waves*, using the story of Jonah as a framing device for the collection. His works—including poetry, nonfiction, fiction, and plays— have appeared in many magazines and journals including *Ethel Zine*, *Borderlands*, *Pilgrimage Press*, *Poetry Quarterly*, and *Sandpiper*. He is a full-time English professor in Plano, Texas.

Linnea Orians is pursuing writing and editing to make the world feel a bit smaller and much sweeter. She believes relationships are one of the greatest ways to be a light, and truly loves how God reveals himself through his Word. Linnea and her husband live in

Upstate New York looking forward to multiple cups of morning coffee and the smell of snow. To follow her writing journey, she is on Instagram @linesbylinnea.

Ashley C. Shannon is a wife, mother, and adventure curator. As a lifelong learner, she enjoys exploring the Midwest where she lives and painting her experience of motherhood with words. You can find her on Instagram at @ashley_c_shannon.

Liz Trujillo is wife to one, mom to three, and a barista & blogger to all. She and her family live in Grand Junction, CO, where she serves on staff at Junction Community Church. On the list of Liz's favorite things is the song, "My Favorite Things", coffee in all forms, traveling with her family, and connecting over conversation. Most days, you'll find her standing up typing with an iced coffee in hand or singing songs to Jesus.

Ashlee Spear is a Spanish teacher and mom to two young girls. She writes from Southern California. She loves reading, running, collecting vintage fashion magazines, and enjoying a cocktail after work with her husband. Find her on Instagram @ashleespear.

Peter Lilly is a British Poet who grew up in Gloucester before spending eight years in London studying theology and working with the homeless. He now lives in the South of France with his wife and son, where he concentrates on writing, teaching English, and community building. His recent and forthcoming publications include Dreich, Wine Cellar Press, Green Ink Poetry, Macrina, The Minison Project, and Paddler Press. His debut Collection 'An Array of Vapour' is forthcoming with TSL publications.

Joy A. Mead is a Jesus-loving, American mother living in the United Kingdom with her British husband and their two wonderful children. Author of *Taking Care of Mama: Learning to Look After Yourself While Simultaneously Raising Your Little Ones*, she passionately encourages mothers to be healthier in body, heart, mind, and soul. Joy writes weekly on her blog about journeying with God through everyday life at: www.joyamead.com.

Laura Trimble writes, bakes, and gardens outside Portland, Oregon. A former high school English teacher, she now homeschools her three sons. Her writing has been published by the Rabbit Room and Humane Pursuits and appears on Instagram at @trimblepoetry.

Jennifer Wier is a writer, counselor, and follower of Jesus dedicated to pointing people's hearts toward Home. After earning a master's degree in counseling psychology from Trinity Evangelical Divinity School, she worked with clergy, university students, teen mothers, and community members in need of mental health support until becoming a stay-at-home mom. A Chicago native turned military spouse, Jennifer currently resides in Alaska with her husband of fifteen years and their four young children. She writes regularly at www.jenniferwier.com, where she encourages her readers to embrace both the sweet, sweet grace of God and his call to holiness.

A.M. Everett lives with her darling husband and three precious kids in a country thousands of miles away. She is a disability, homeschool, and TCK Mom, and has so much more to learn about God's good character through the life He's given her. A.M. loves writing, cultivating the plants on her veranda, and drinking no less than three cups of coffee a day.

Ravanna Dee Steinke is a Christian writer, published poet, and homemaker from Minnesota. As a wife and mother to both living and lost children, she shares passionately about them and Jesus in her writing. Her blog is also inspired by an Early Childhood degree and her interest in development and Montessori education.

Elizabeth Wickland lives in Bozeman, Montana with her husband, daughter, and two Yorkies. She has a love for words and their stories and has responded to life through poetry and art for as long as she can remember. She also enjoys gardening and cultivating beauty in her small corner of the world. Her work has been published in The Unmooring, Riveted Literary, and She is Kindred, and you can find her on Instagram at @punamulta.priory and at elizabethwickland.substack.com.

Sarah Soltis is a writer and editor splitting her time between Pennsylvania and Maryland. She currently serves as Managing Editor of Front Porch Republic, and she has published work in *Plough*, *Ekstasis*, and elsewhere.

Deborah Rutherford is a Christian writer-blogger, poet, and Emmy recipient winner makeup artist. She shares her transformative life of Jesus' healing and love on her blog at www.deborahrutherford.com as well as on social media. Deborah writes for Kingdom Edge Magazine, Alethia Today Magazine, and Gracefully Truthful Ministries. You can find her devotional in the new book "Shepherd on Duty: Promises of God you Can Trust."

Jessica Mangano lives in Connecticut with her husband, celebrating God's imagination through writing and photography. Jessica turns towards writing to better understand the relationship between joy and suffering as a follower of Christ, an interest stemming from her mother's stubborn faith in the face of progressive and chronic illness.

Marilyn Gardner is a writer and public health nurse living in Boston, Massachusetts. Marilyn writes about communicating across the boundaries of faith and culture on her blog Communicating Across Boundaries. She is also the author of two books: *Between Worlds: Essays on Culture & Belonging* and *Worlds Apart: A Third Culture Kid's Journey*. You can also find her writing at Plough Magazine, Fathom Magazine, Among Worlds Magazine, and the A Life Overseas Community. Marilyn loves her passport, her family, and God in reverse order. You can find her on Instagram @communicatingacrossboundaries.

Dawn Kopa is an itinerant preacher, Bible teacher, and founder of the book publishing company, Aletheia Press (www.aletheiapressbooks.com), which serves to compel people toward faith in God through the power of the written word. She resides in Houston, TX, and likes to live with the doors to her home and her heart wide open.

Veronica Maria Jarski is a first-generation American, the daughter of Argentine immigrants who primarily spoke Spanish at home. She learned English through immersion and copious viewings of "Sesame Street" and "Mr. Rogers' Neighborhood" episodes. Years later, she has a career saturated in wordsmithing: newspaper reporter, proofreader, editorial assistant, editor, content writer, senior content writer, freelance writer, editorial project manager, and managing editor. Veronica's written work has spanned all types of content, including long-form articles, ebooks, how-to guides, opinion pieces, poems, and scripts.

Annie Nardone is a writer for *Cultivating Magazine*, a travel blogger for Clarendon Press U.K., and Managing Editor and author for *An Unexpected Journal*. She collaborated on books published by Square Halo Press and Rabbit Room Press. Annie holds a Master of Arts in Cultural Apologetics and feels passionate about the integration of the arts, humanities, and the Christian imagination.

Madeline Wilkins is a former counselor turned mother turned writer. She lives with her husband and their three children in SC. When she's not wrangling kids, she enjoys writing about their days navigating the joys and difficulties of parenting a child with Autism. Her most recent project was a children's book Gus' Special Magical Most Favorite Hat inspired by her son, Gus. You can find lots of updates on Instagram at @madelinekwilkins as well as on her website www.mkwpoems.com.

Rebecca D. Martin lives with her family in Central Virginia, where she consumes books and tea at an alarming rate, sometimes teaches teenagers American Literature, and weekly feeds bearded dragons at the local nature center. Her essays and poems have been published with the *Curator*, the *Rabbit Room, Tweetspeak Poetry*, and (upcoming) *Taproot* magazine, among others. Her memoir, full of books and houses, will be out with T.S. Poetry Press in Fall 2023, and she can be found at https://rebeccadmartin.substack.com/

Donors

A special thank you to our donors to help publish this journal...

Donna Bucher
Awara Fernandez
Maria Macik
Lee Kiblinger
Mary Anne Abdo
Leslie Jones

Thank You

Thank you to all our talented contributors who have made this literary journal possible. Also, a special thank you to our Communications Coordinator, Leslie Bustard, for her willing heart to serve Calla Press. Thank you to our wonderful editorial assistant, Erin Samples, for her dedicated heart in helping edit this journal. You both are a gift!

Thank you so much to Donna Bucher @serenityinsuffering and Awara Fernandez for donating the final amounts we needed to print this journal.

To God be the glory, forever and ever. Amen.

"Many of our hours of pain and weakness have been lightened by preparing the first volume of our book on the Psalms for the press. If we could not preach we could write, and we pray that this form of service may be accepted of the Lord" (Charles Haddon Spurgeon, *Sword & Trowel*, January 1870).

www.ingramcontent.com/pod-product-compliance
Lightning Source LLC
Chambersburg PA
CBHW020034310726
48970CB00007B/2252